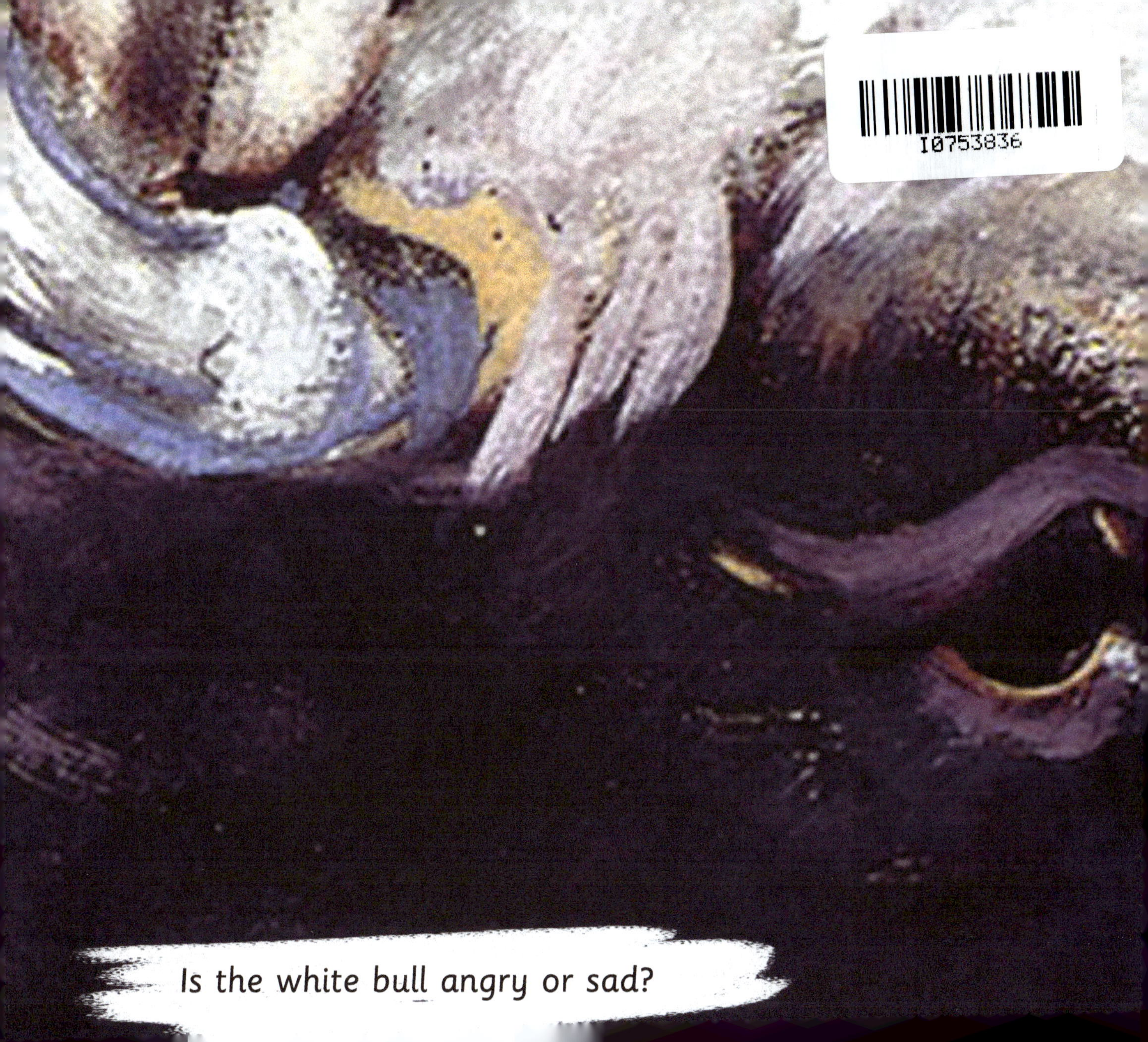
Is the white bull angry or sad?

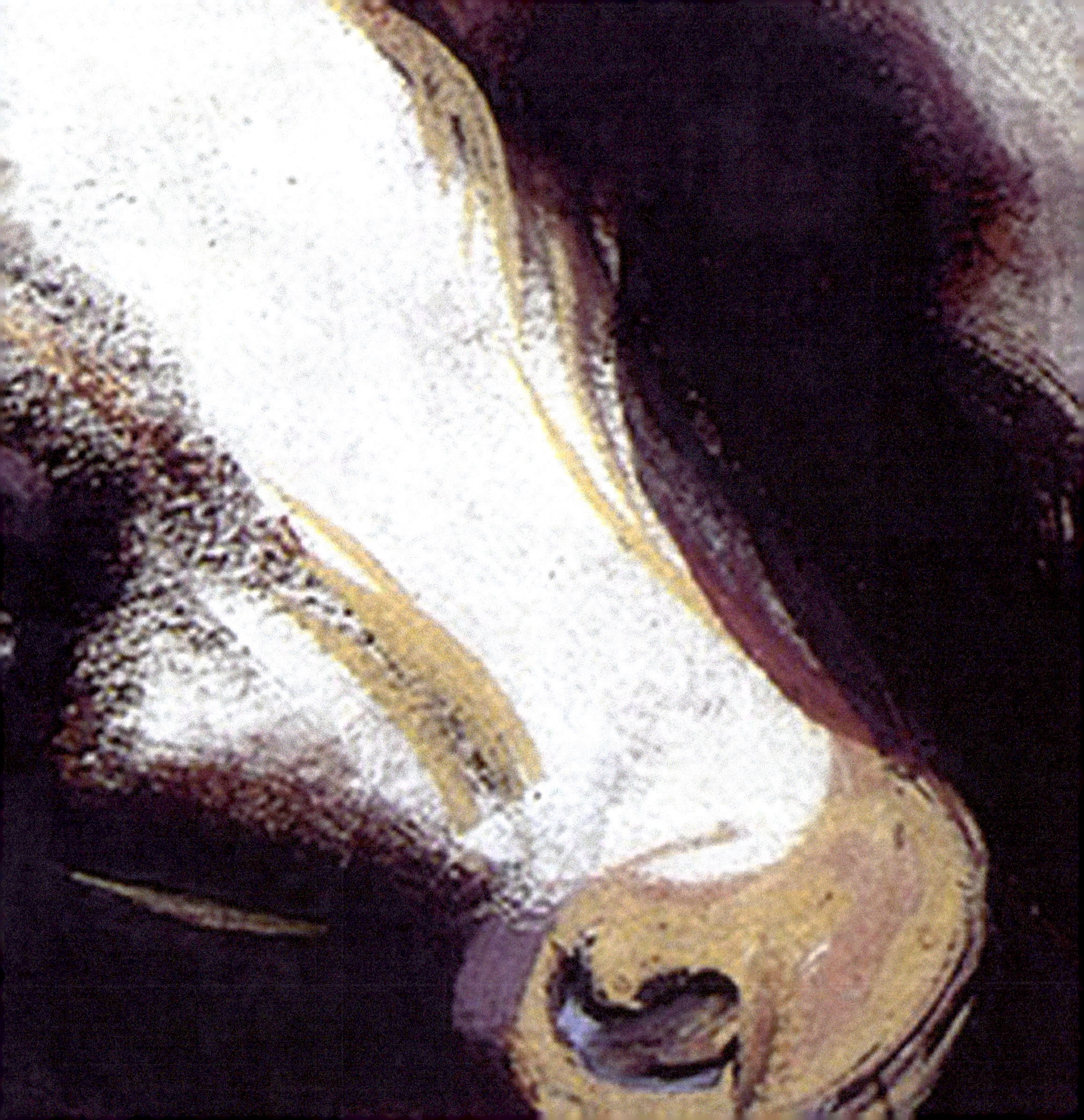

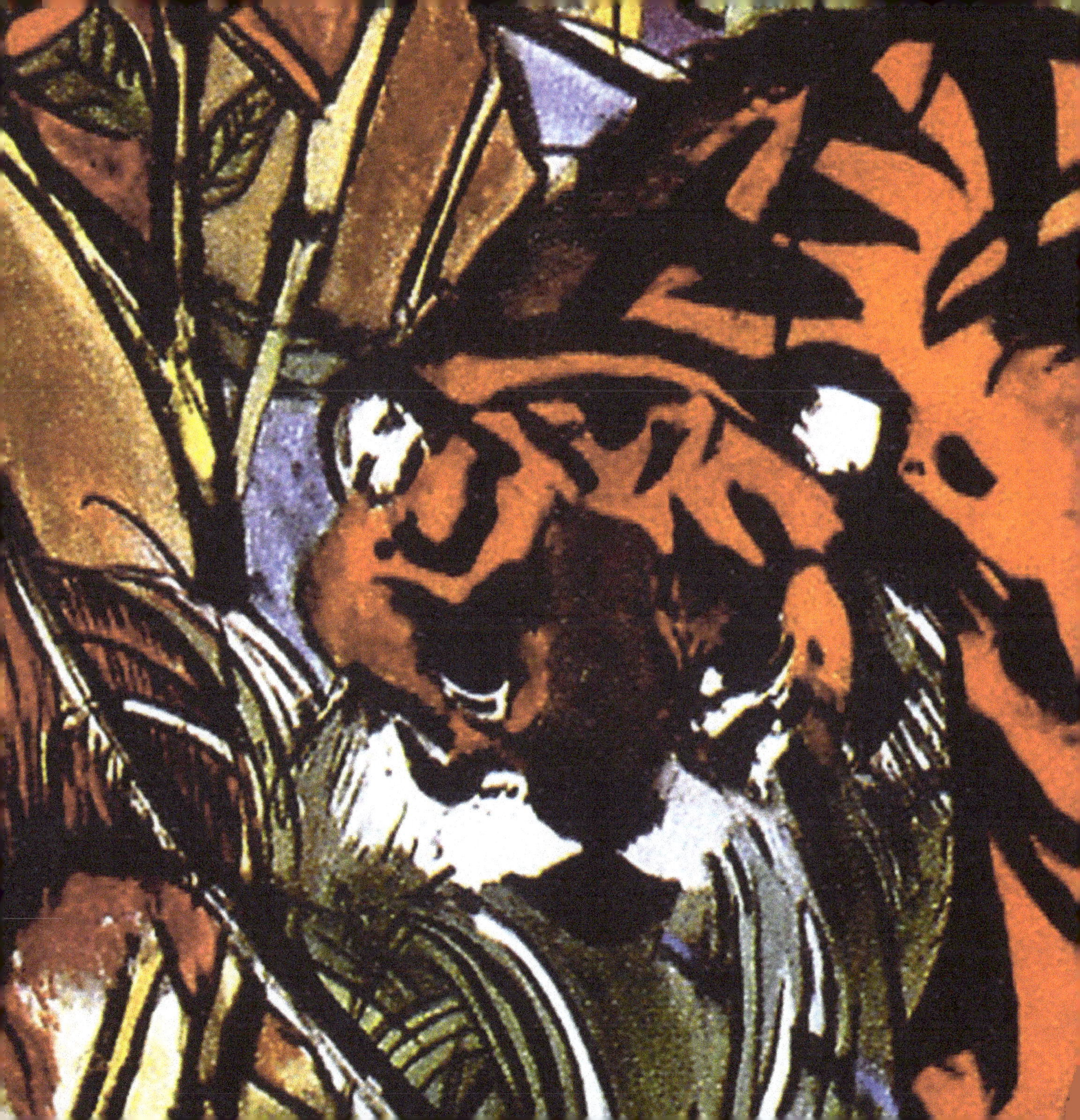

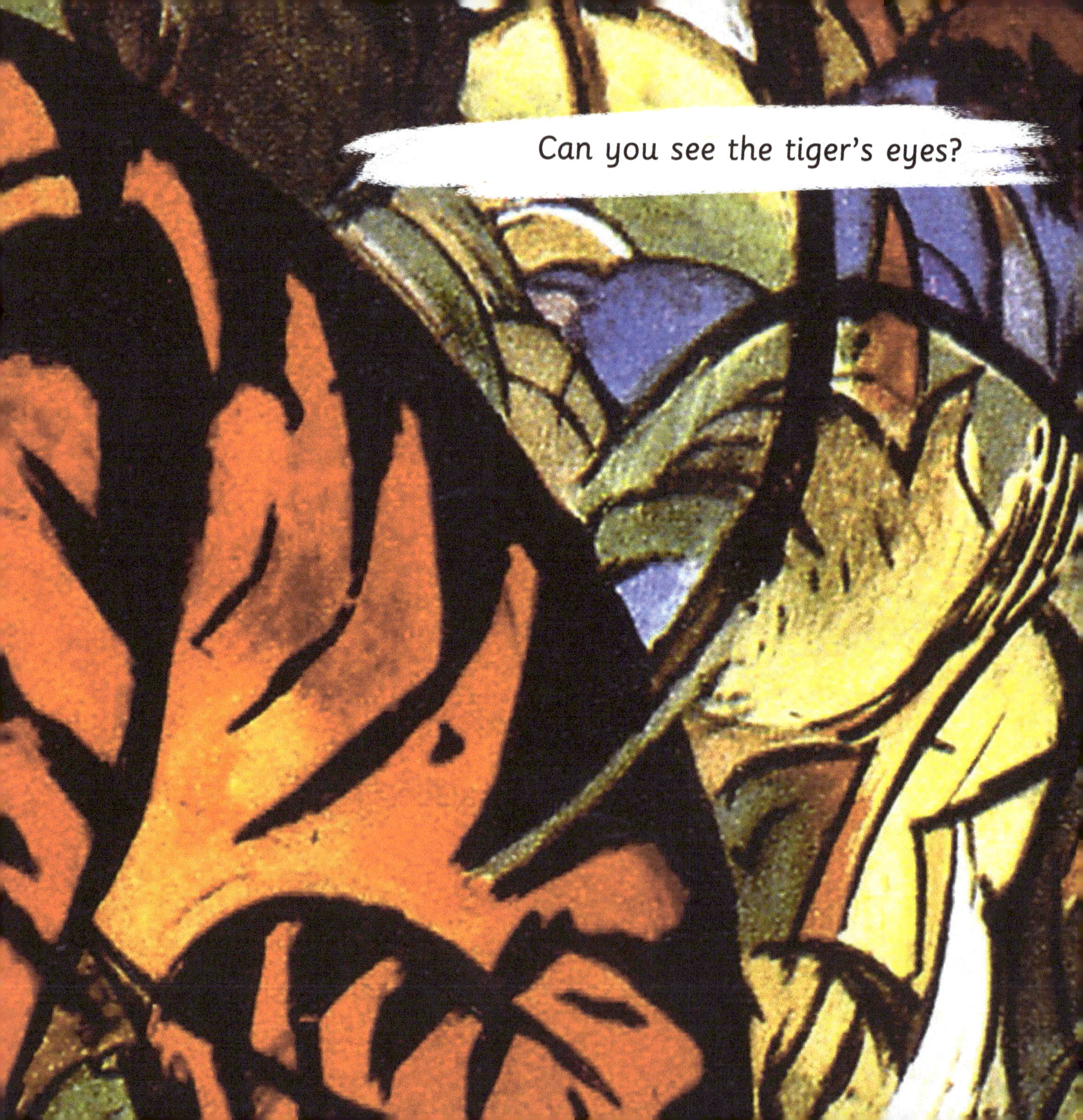

Can you see the tiger's eyes?

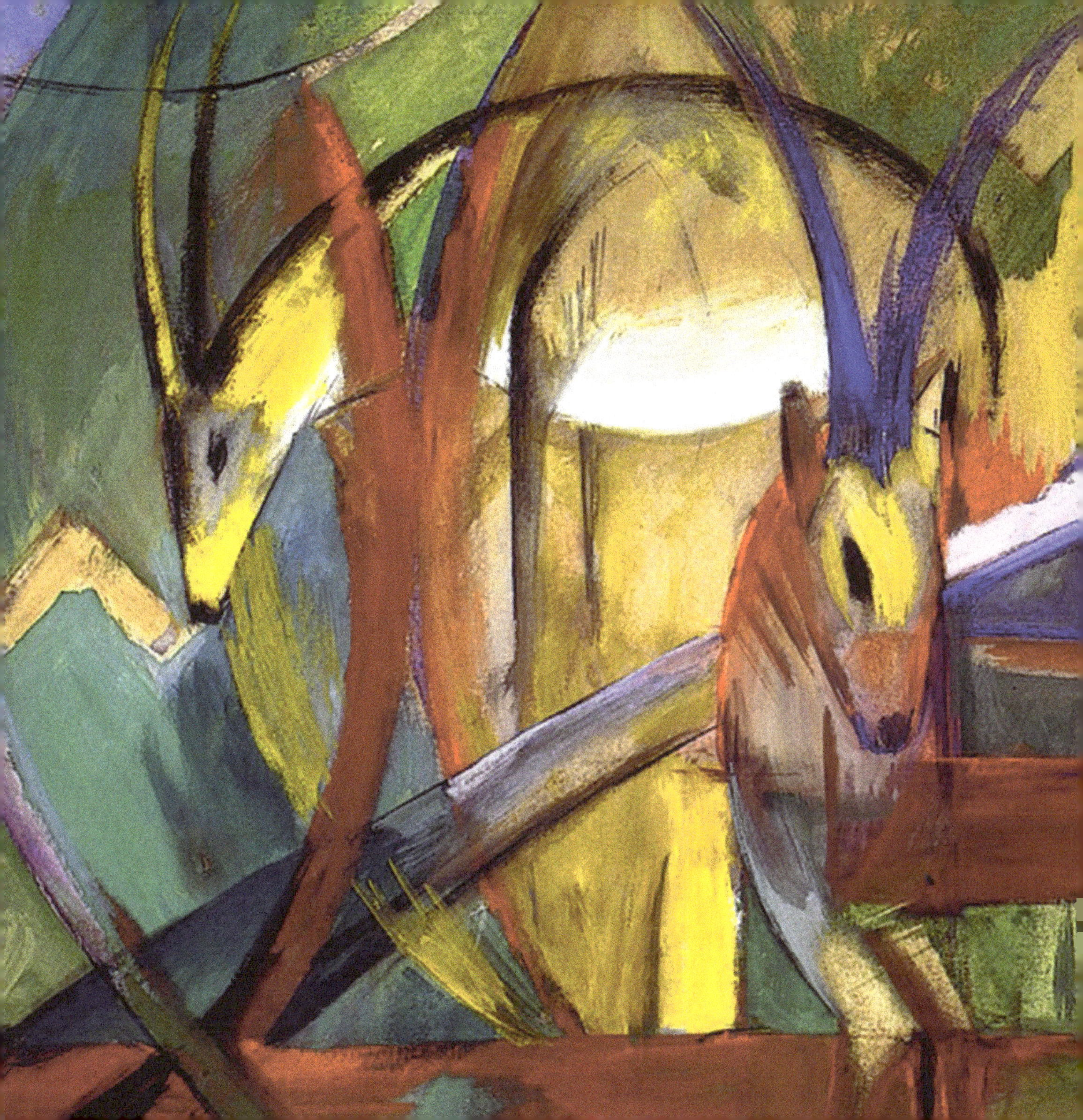

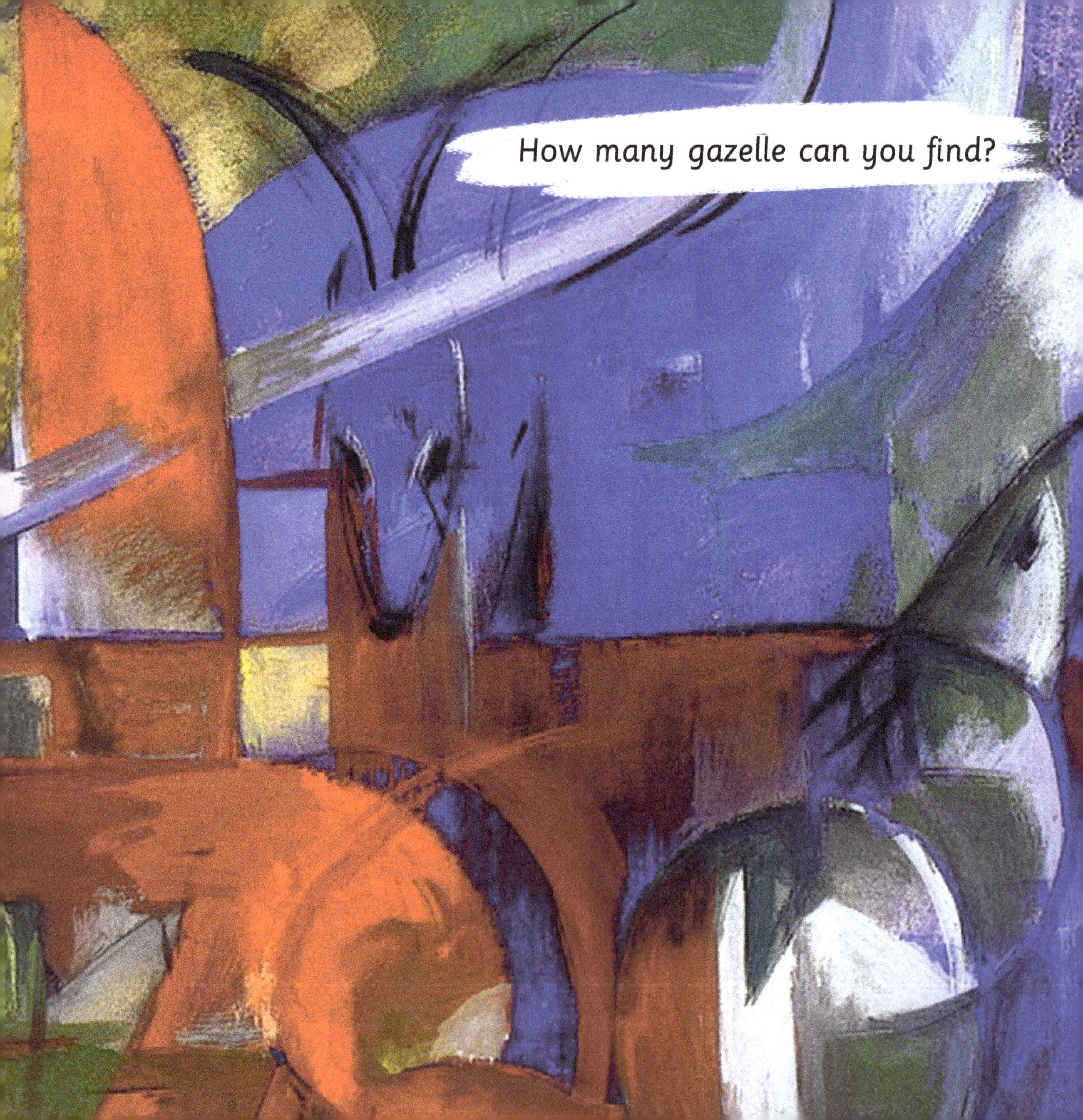
How many gazelle can you find?

Have you seen a yellow cow?

Would a yellow cow give milk?

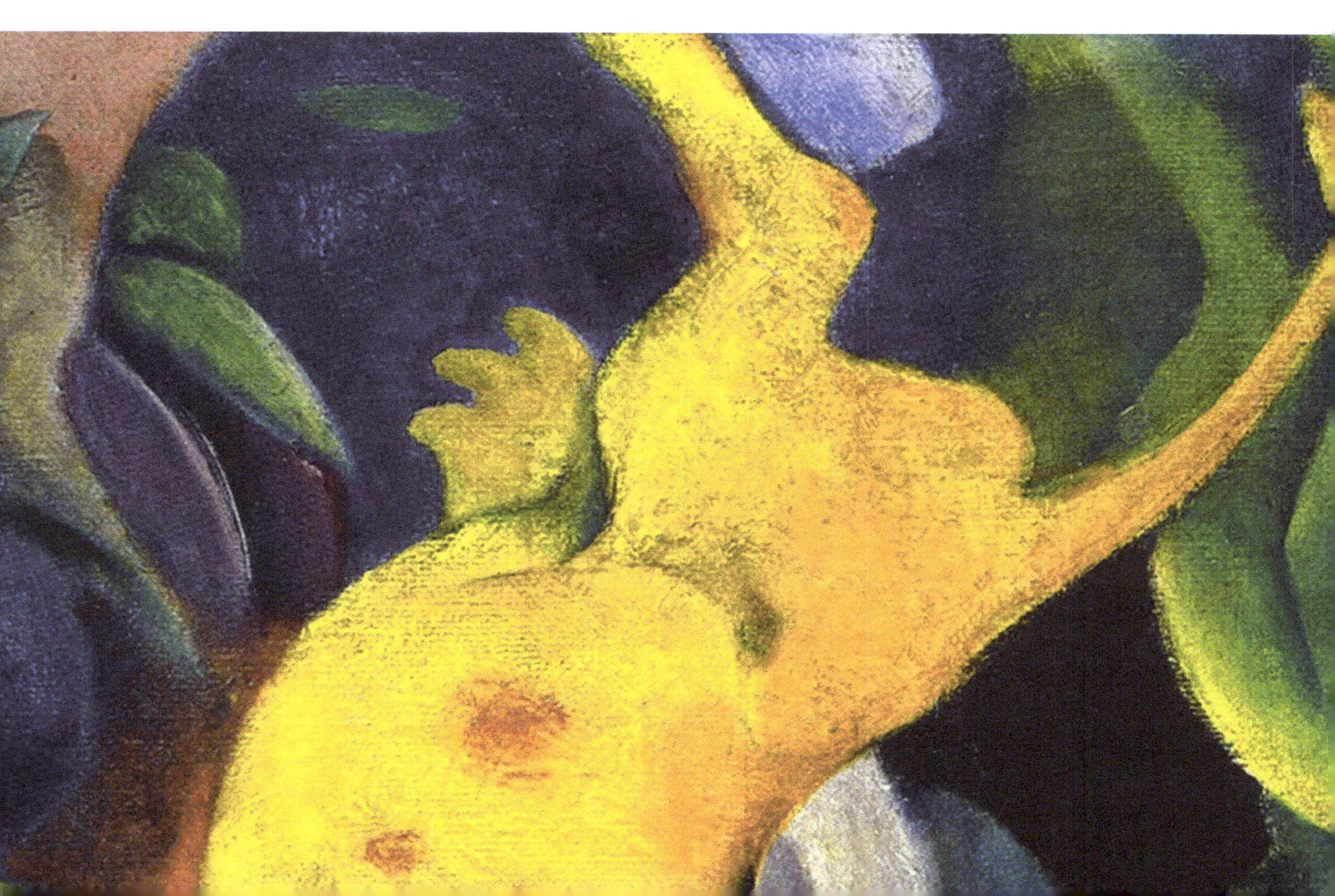

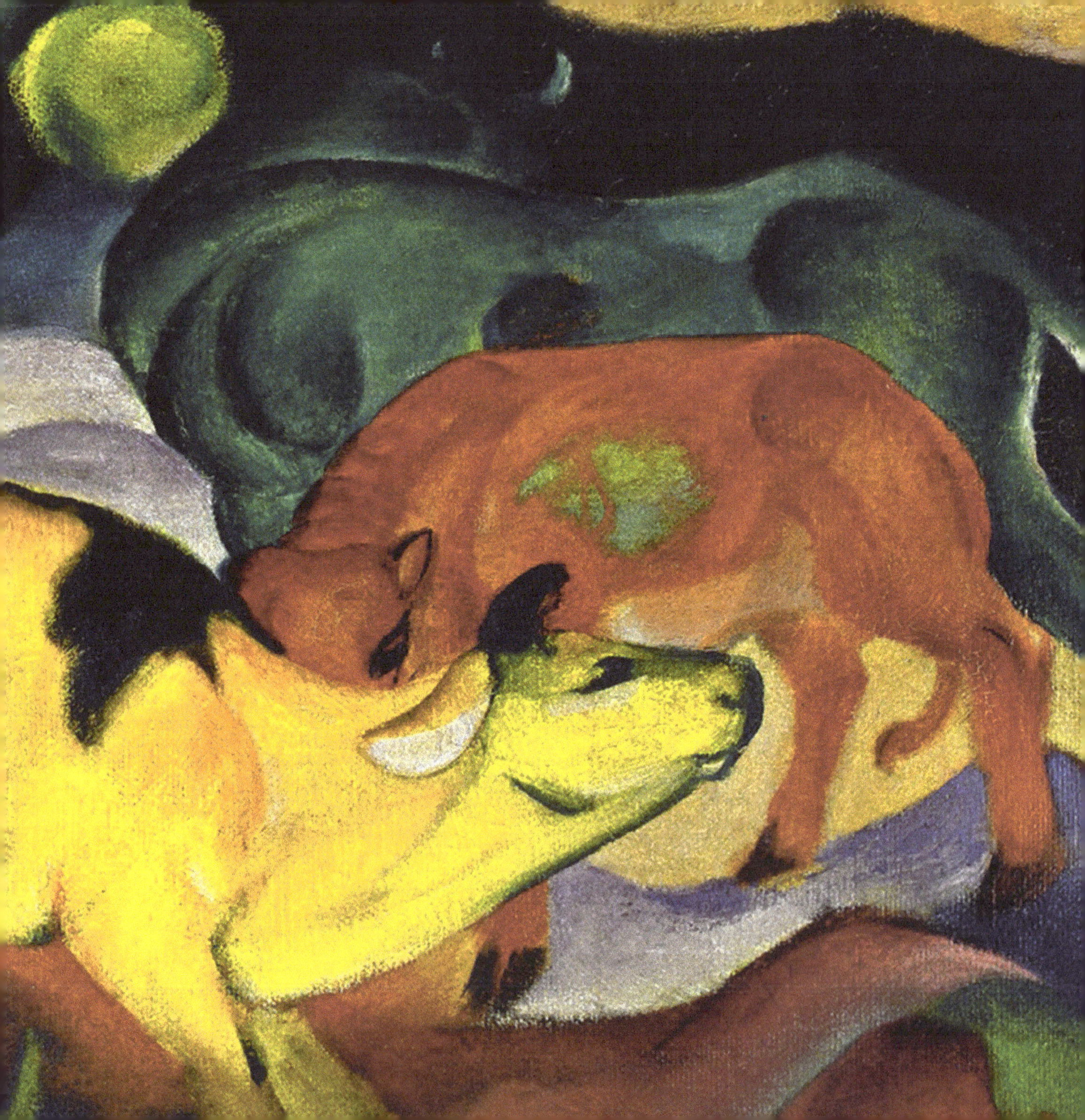

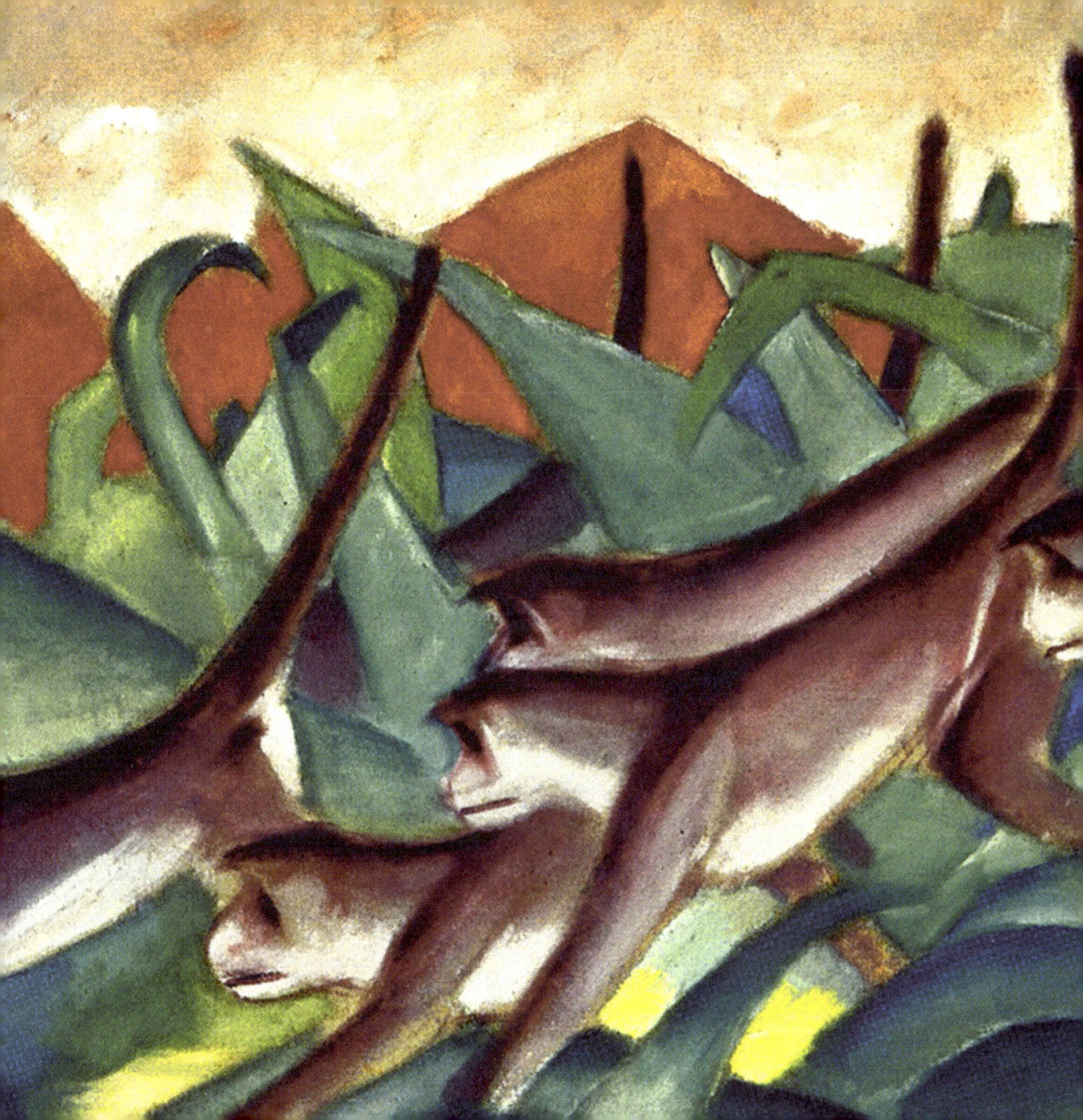

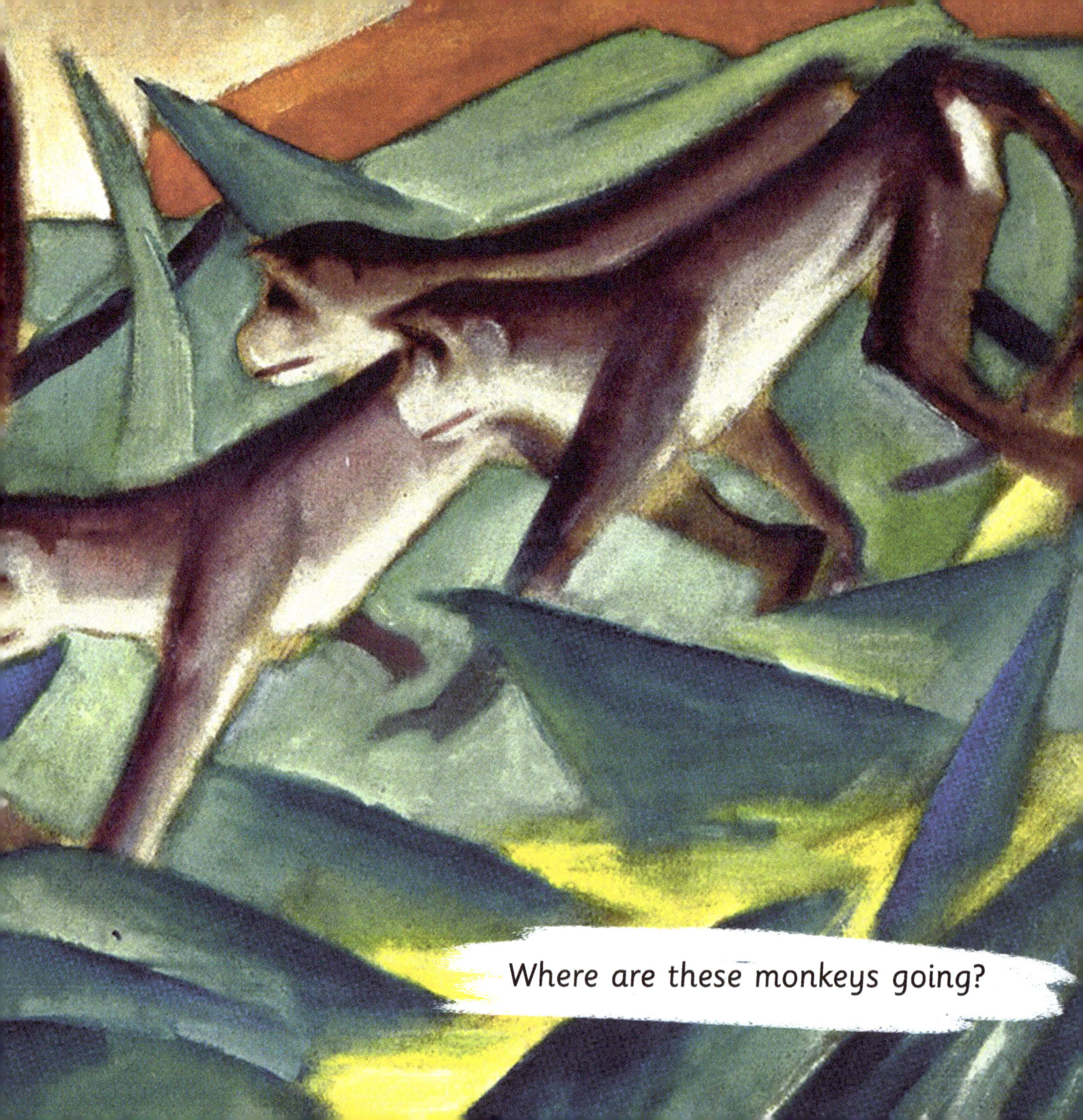

Where are these monkeys going?

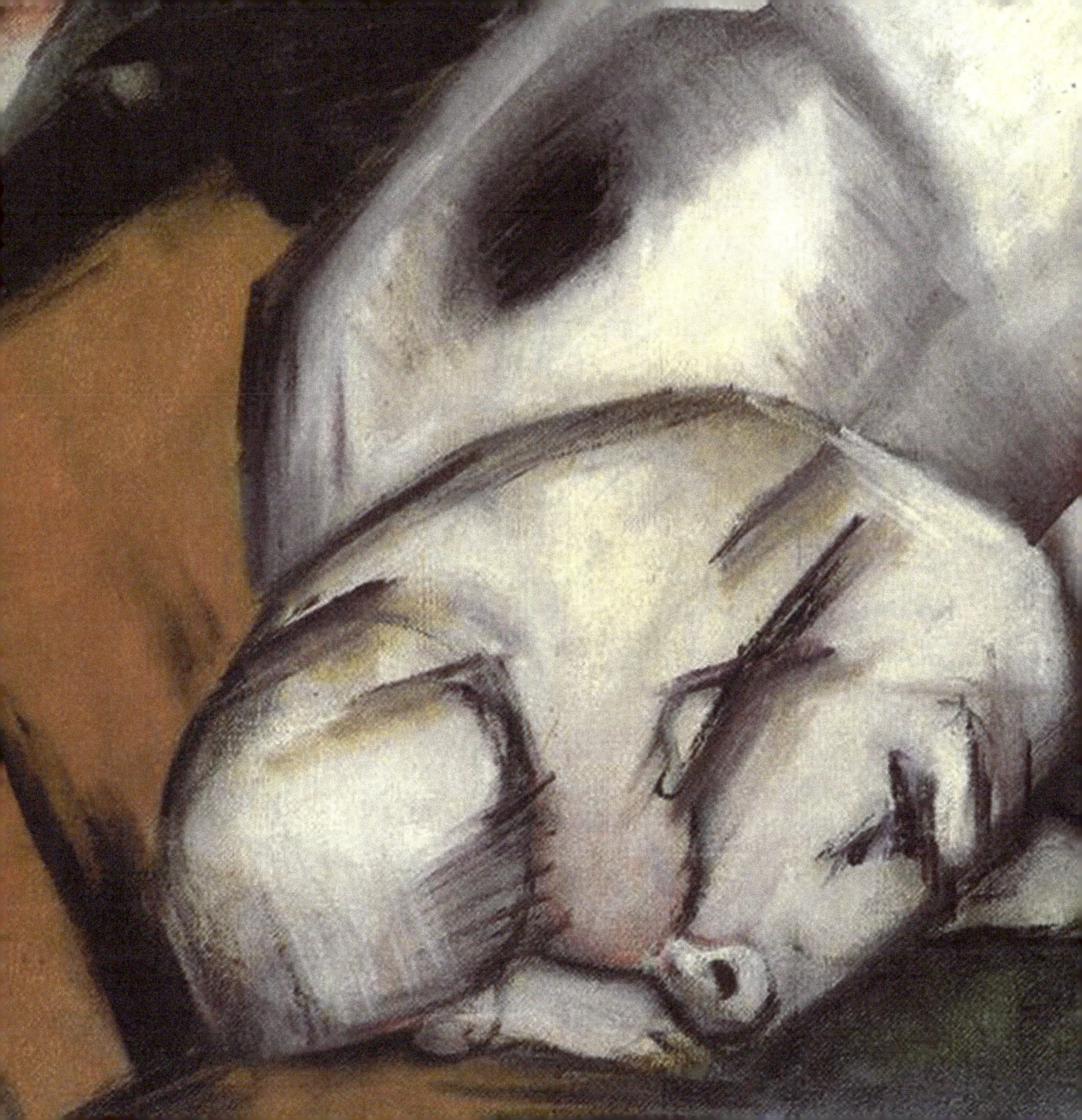

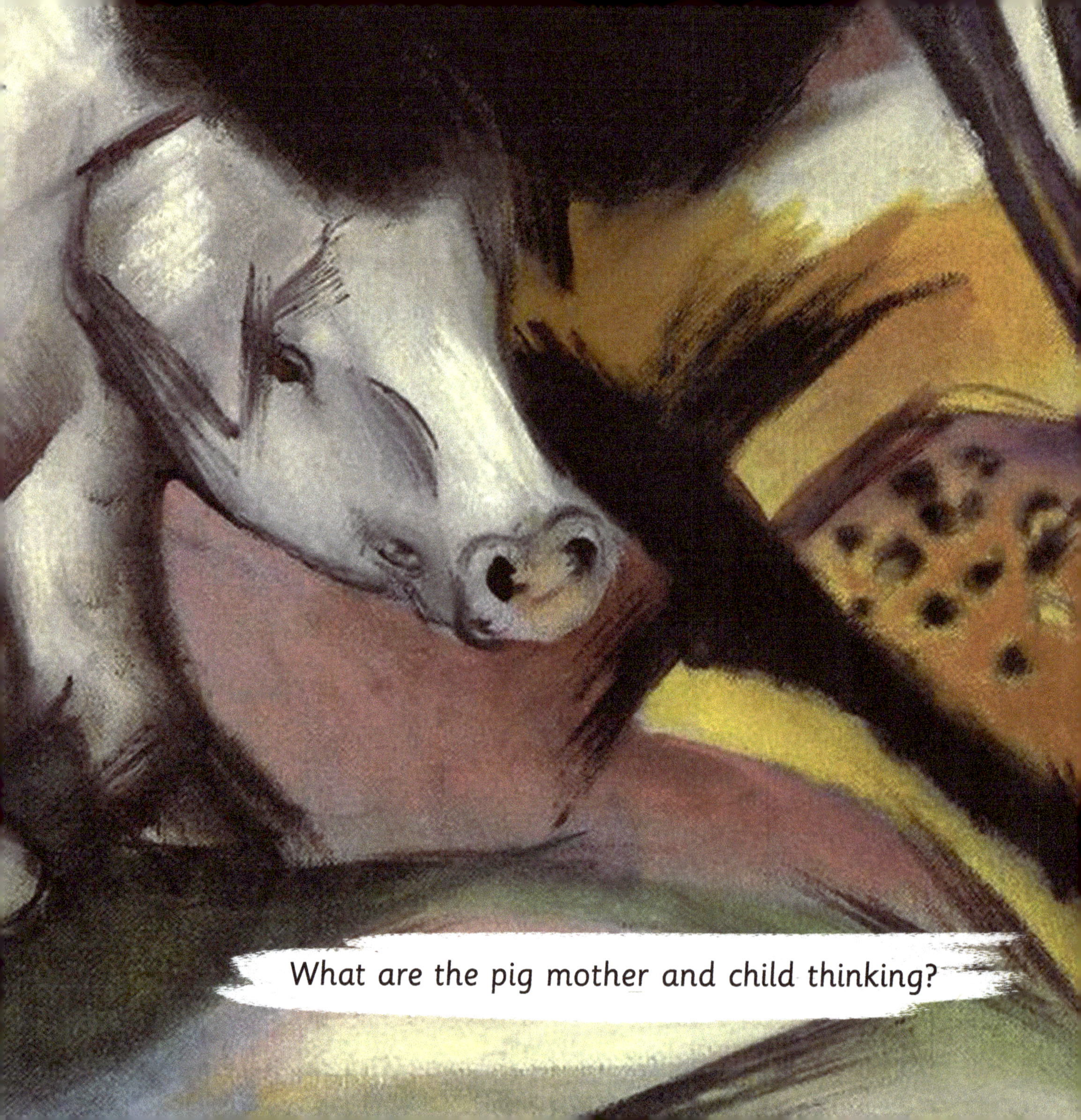

What are the pig mother and child thinking?

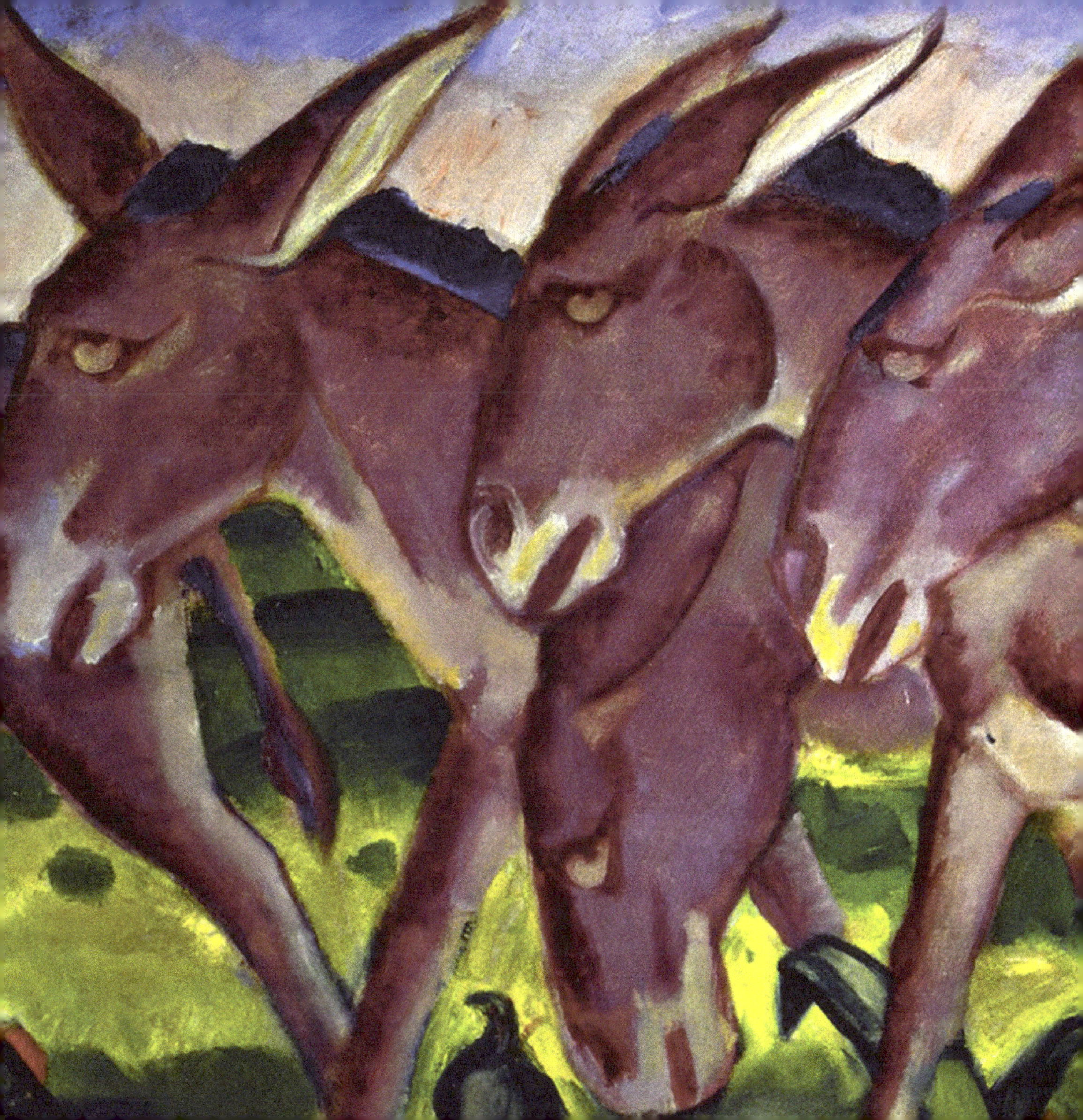

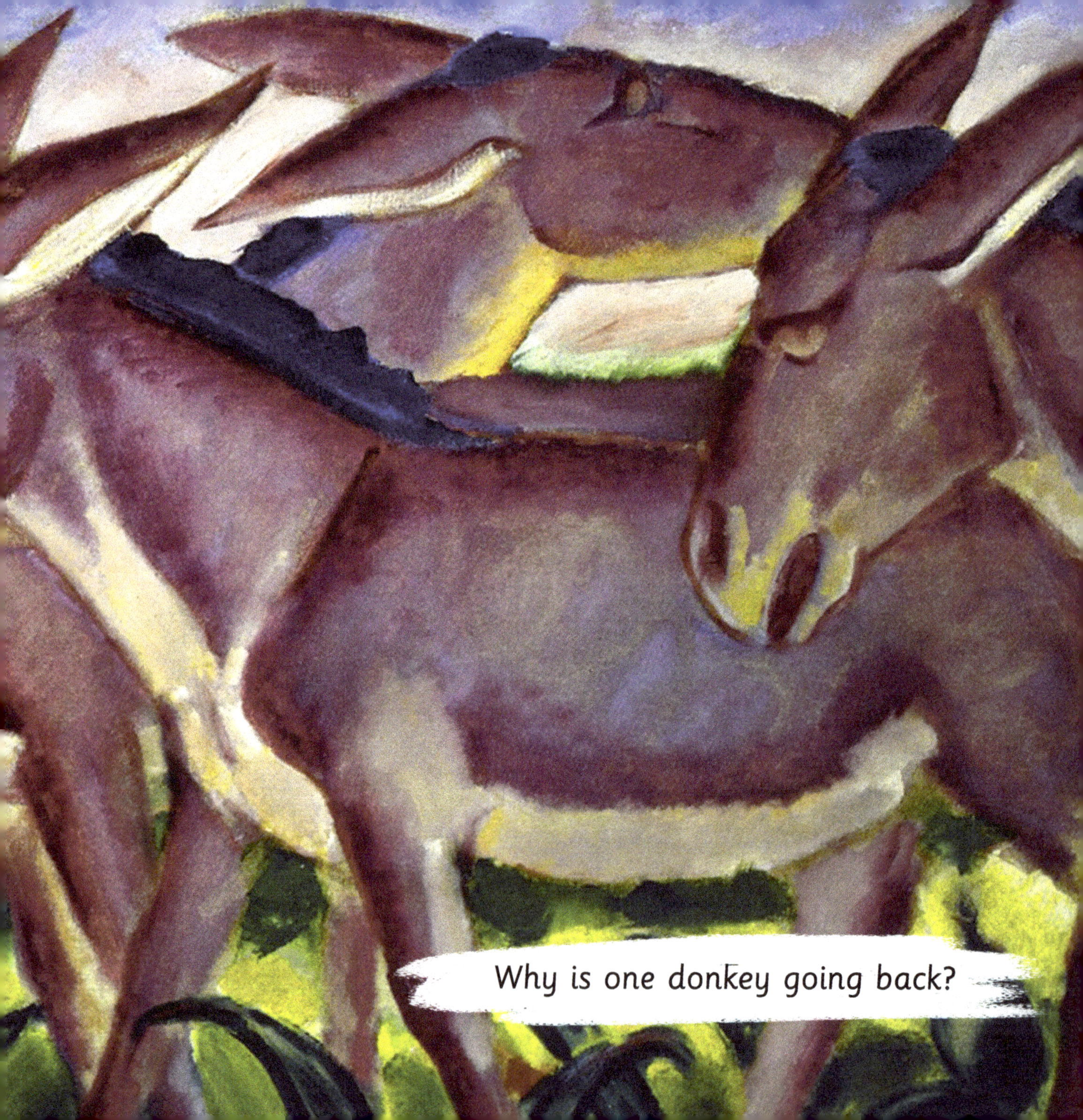

Why is one donkey going back?

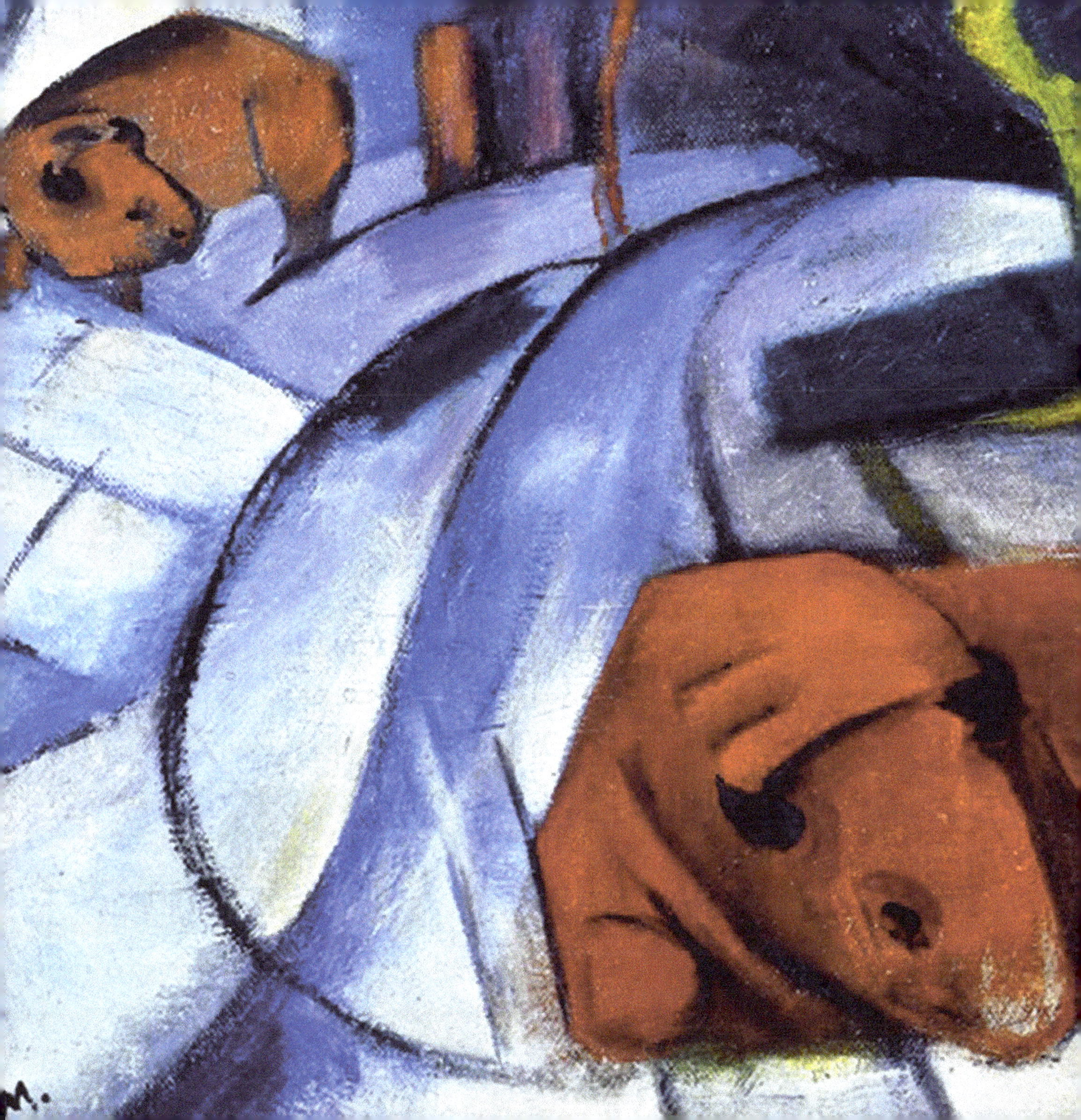

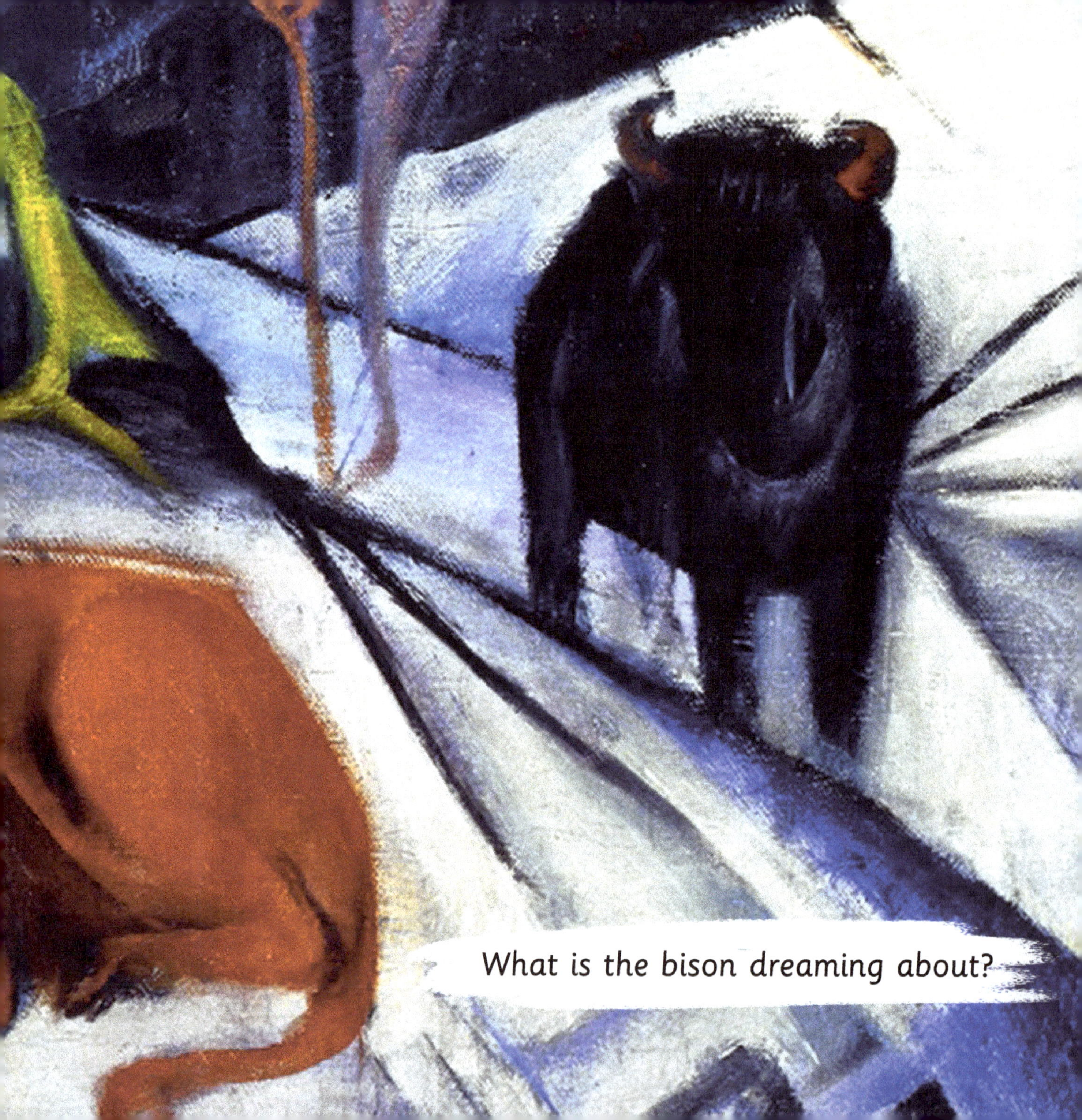

What is the bison dreaming about?

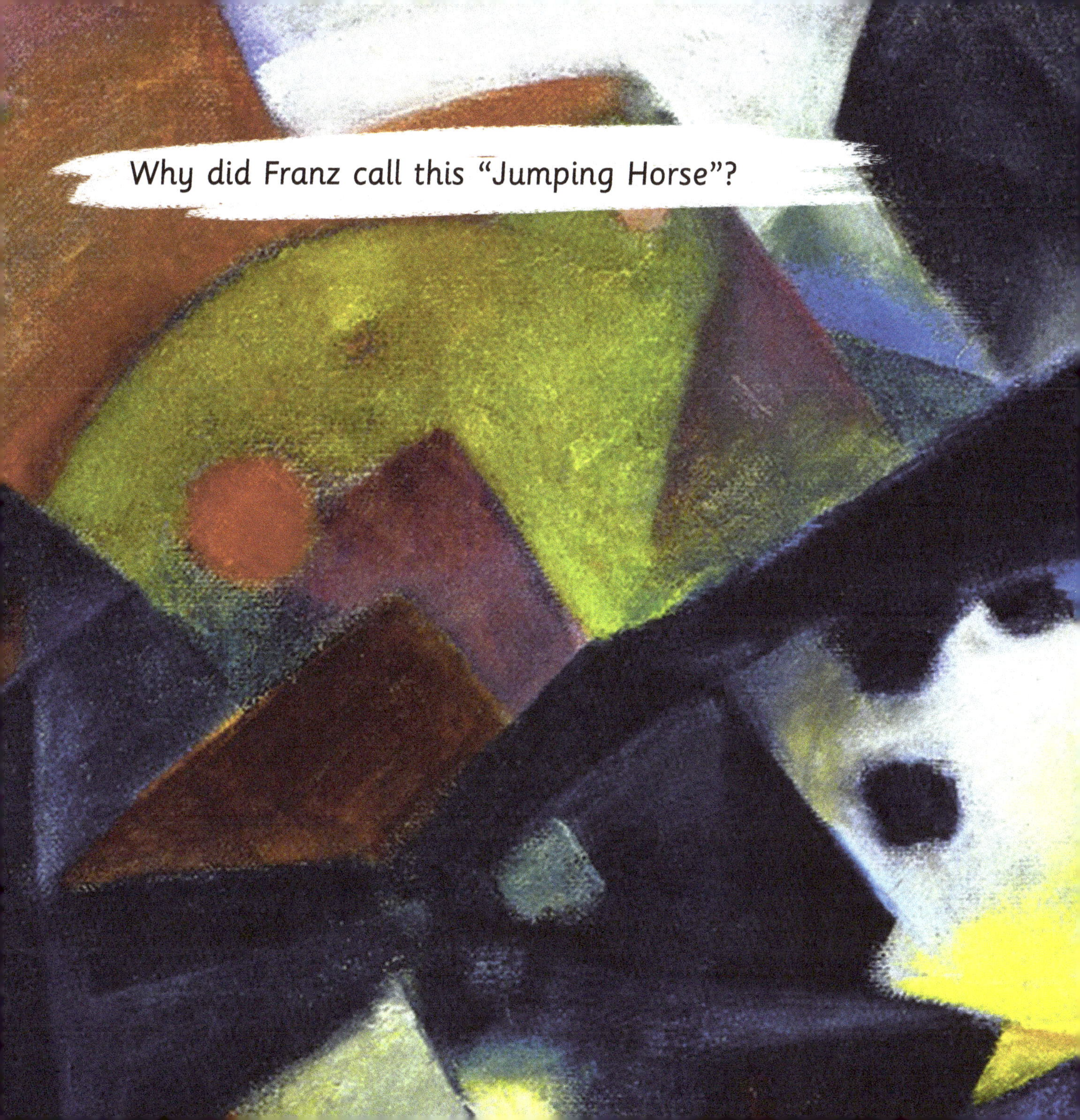

Why did Franz call this “Jumping Horse”?

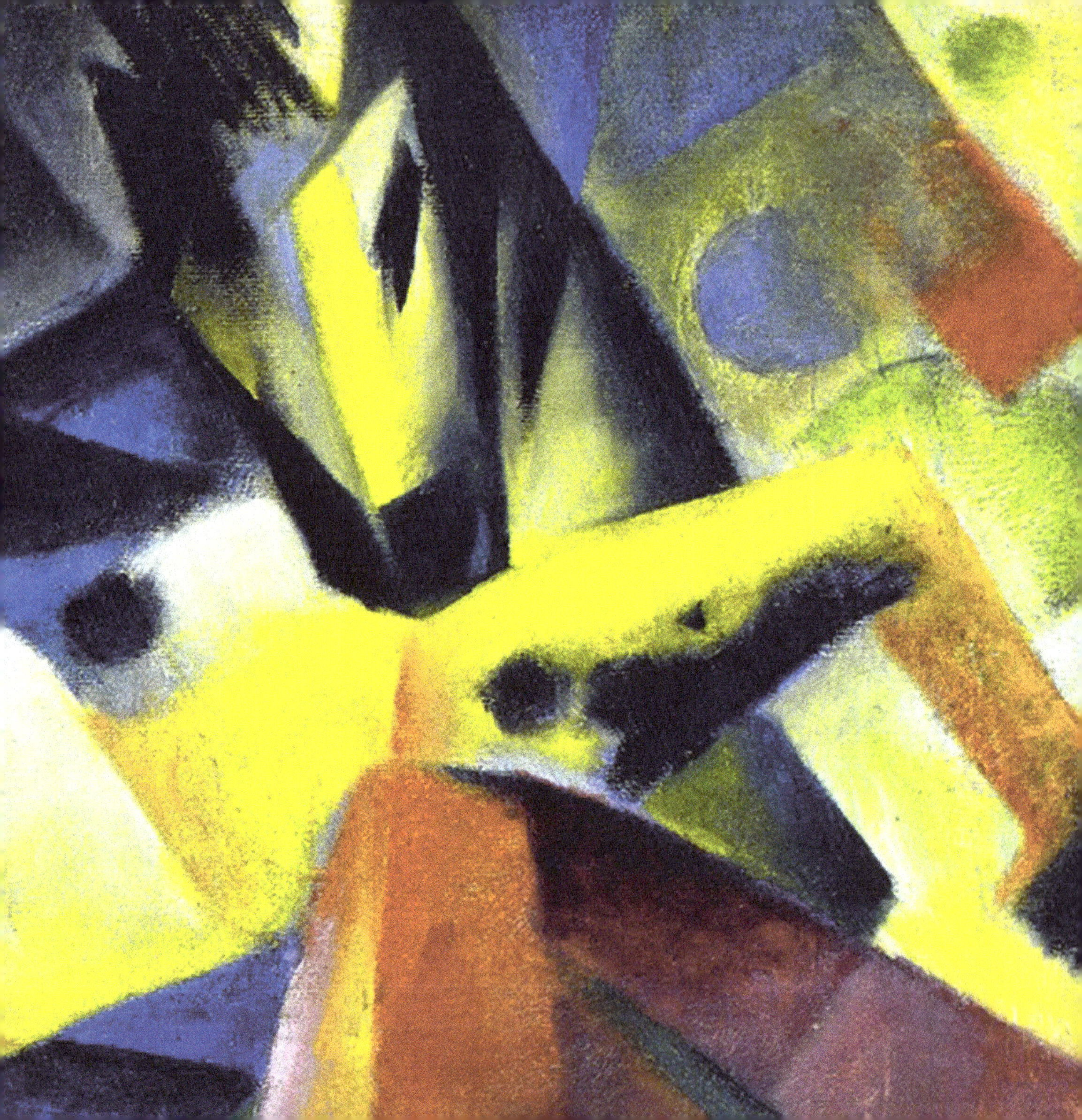

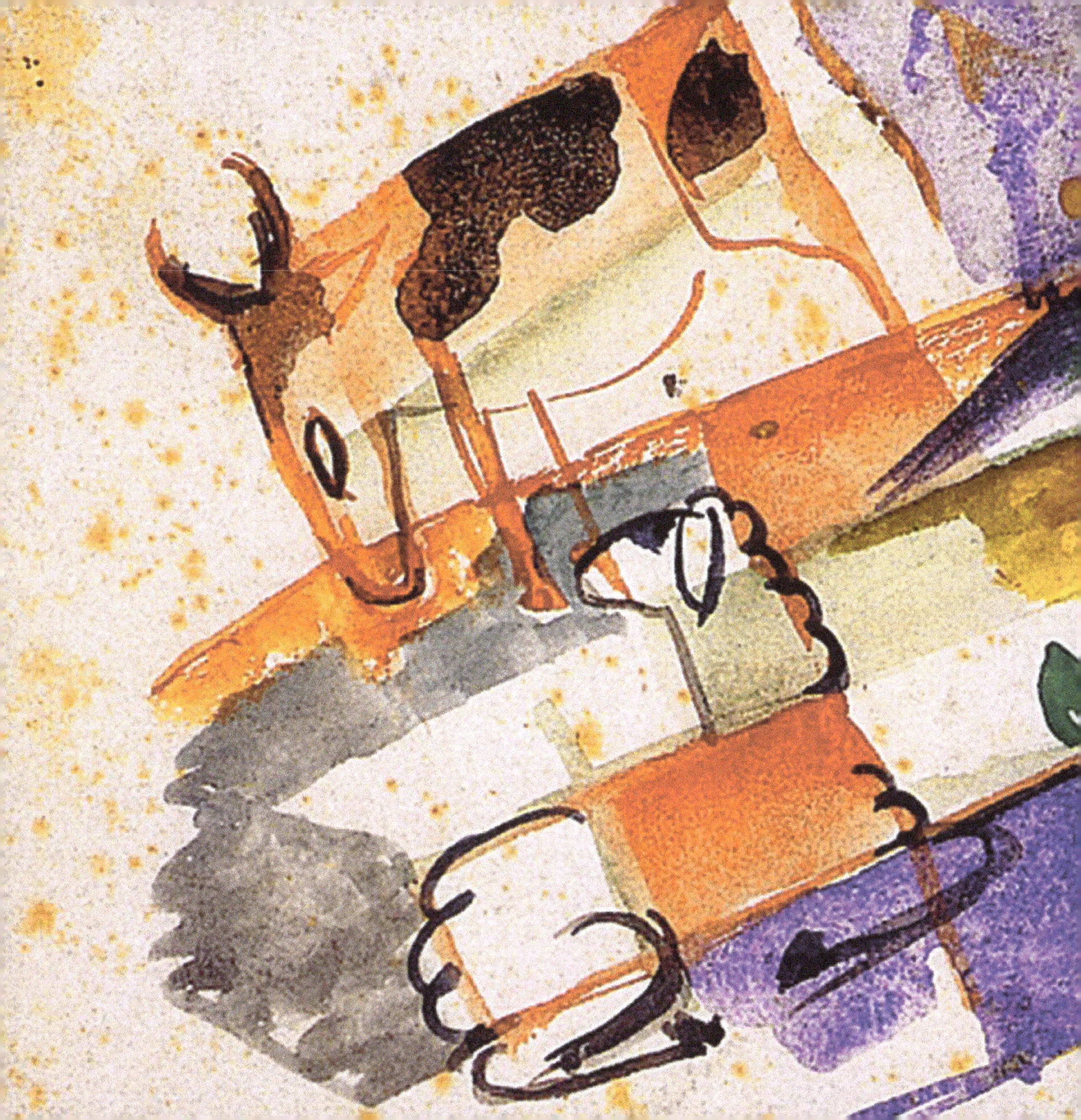

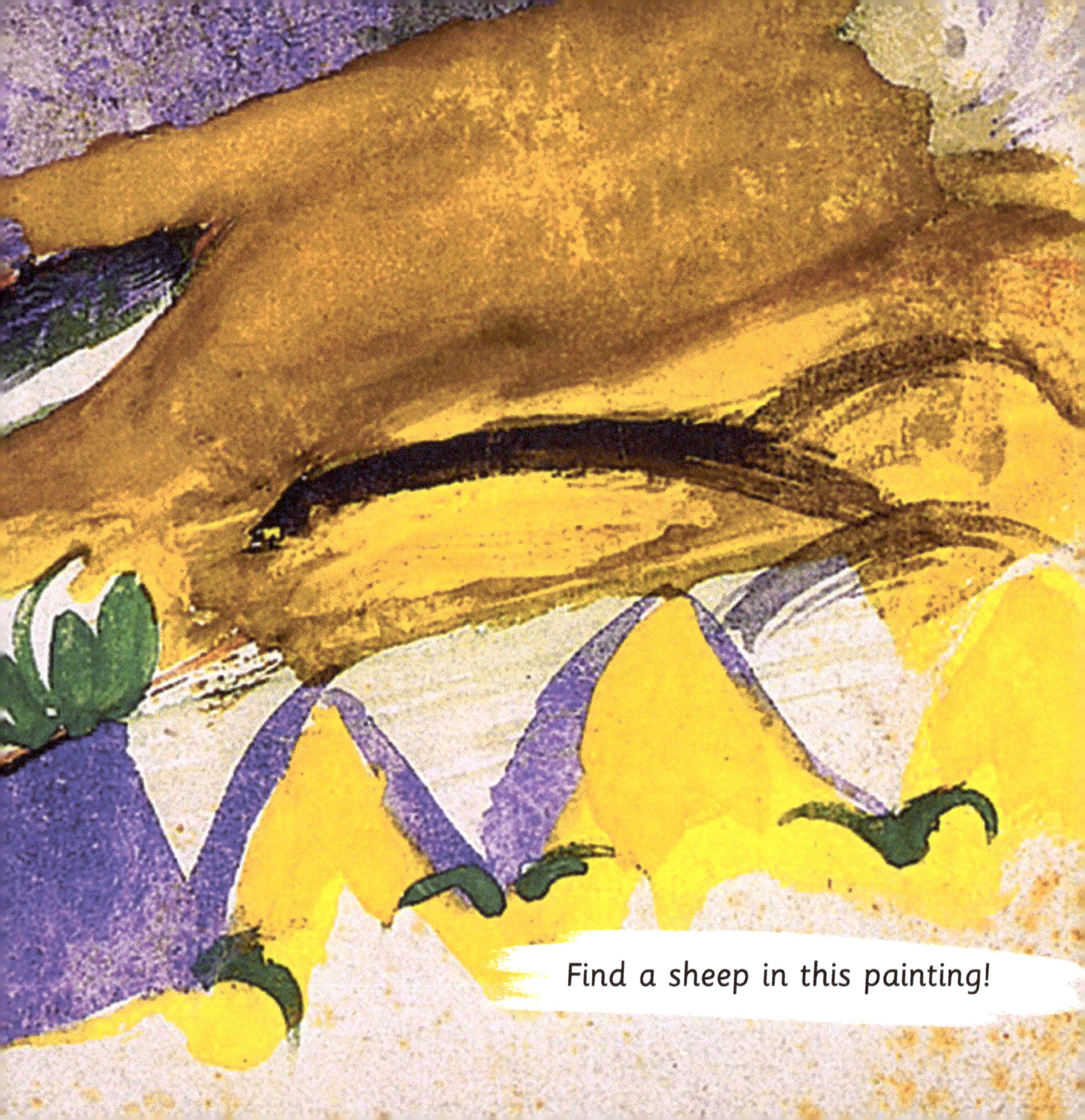

Find a sheep in this painting!

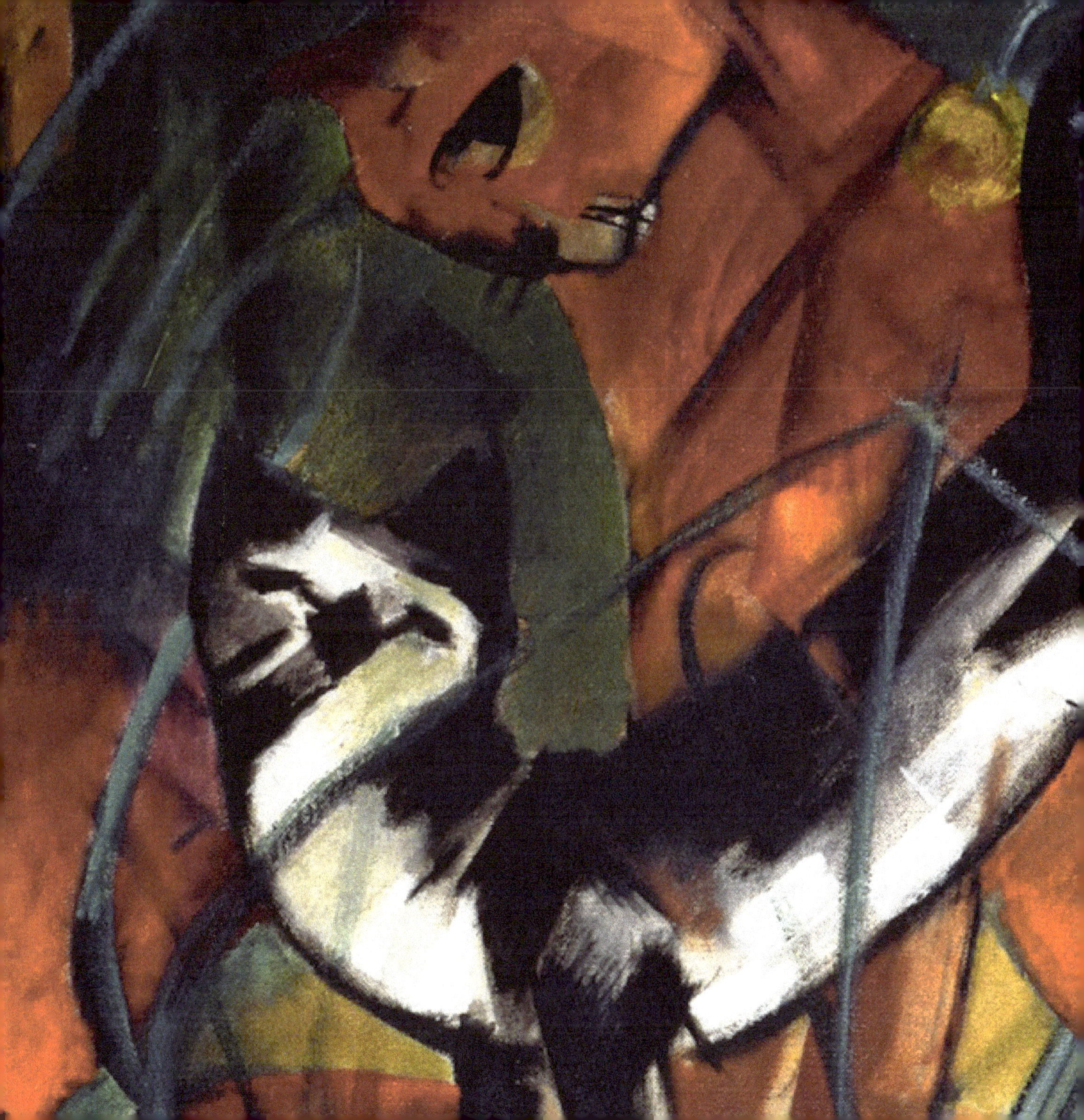

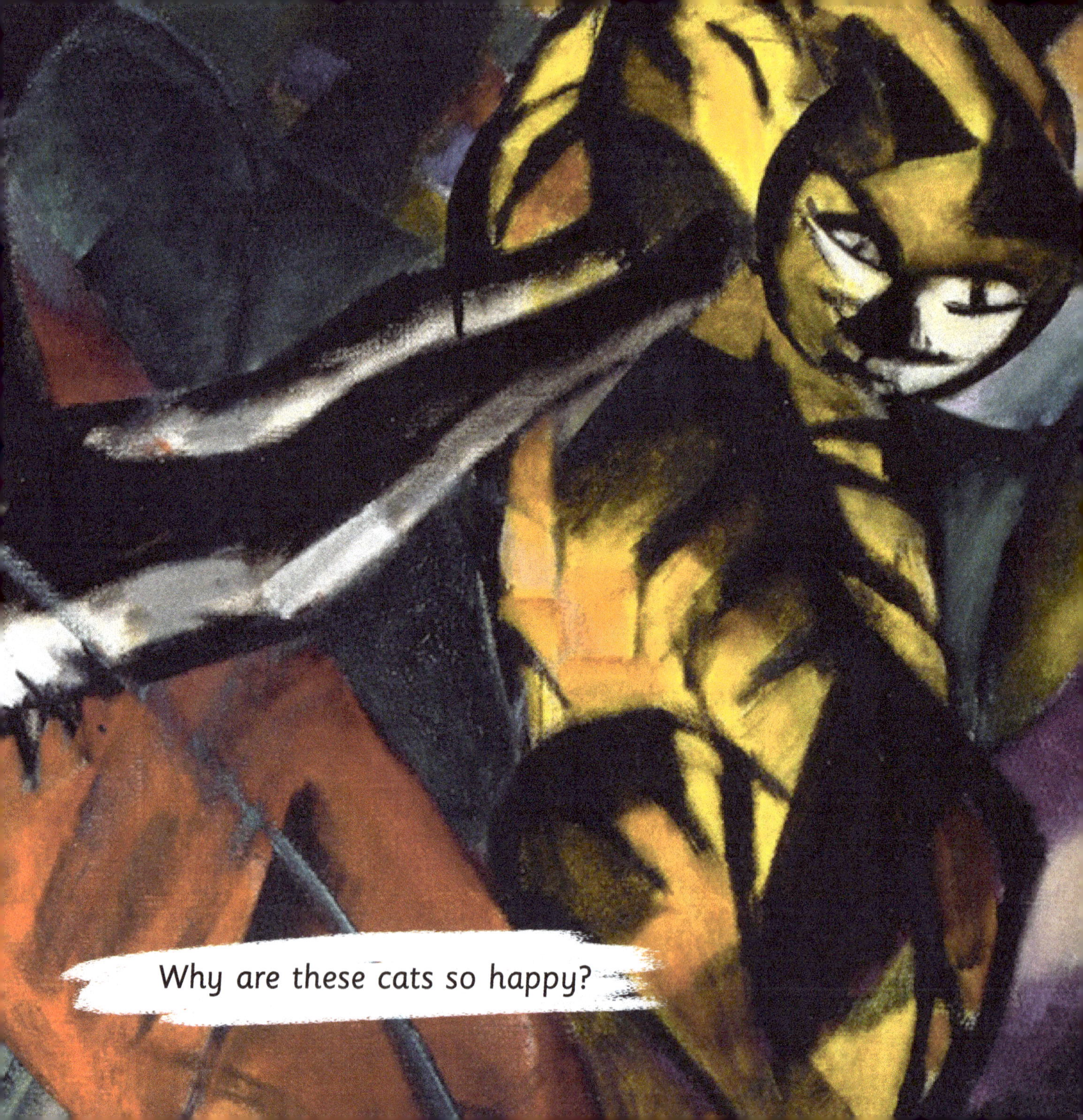

Why are these cats so happy?

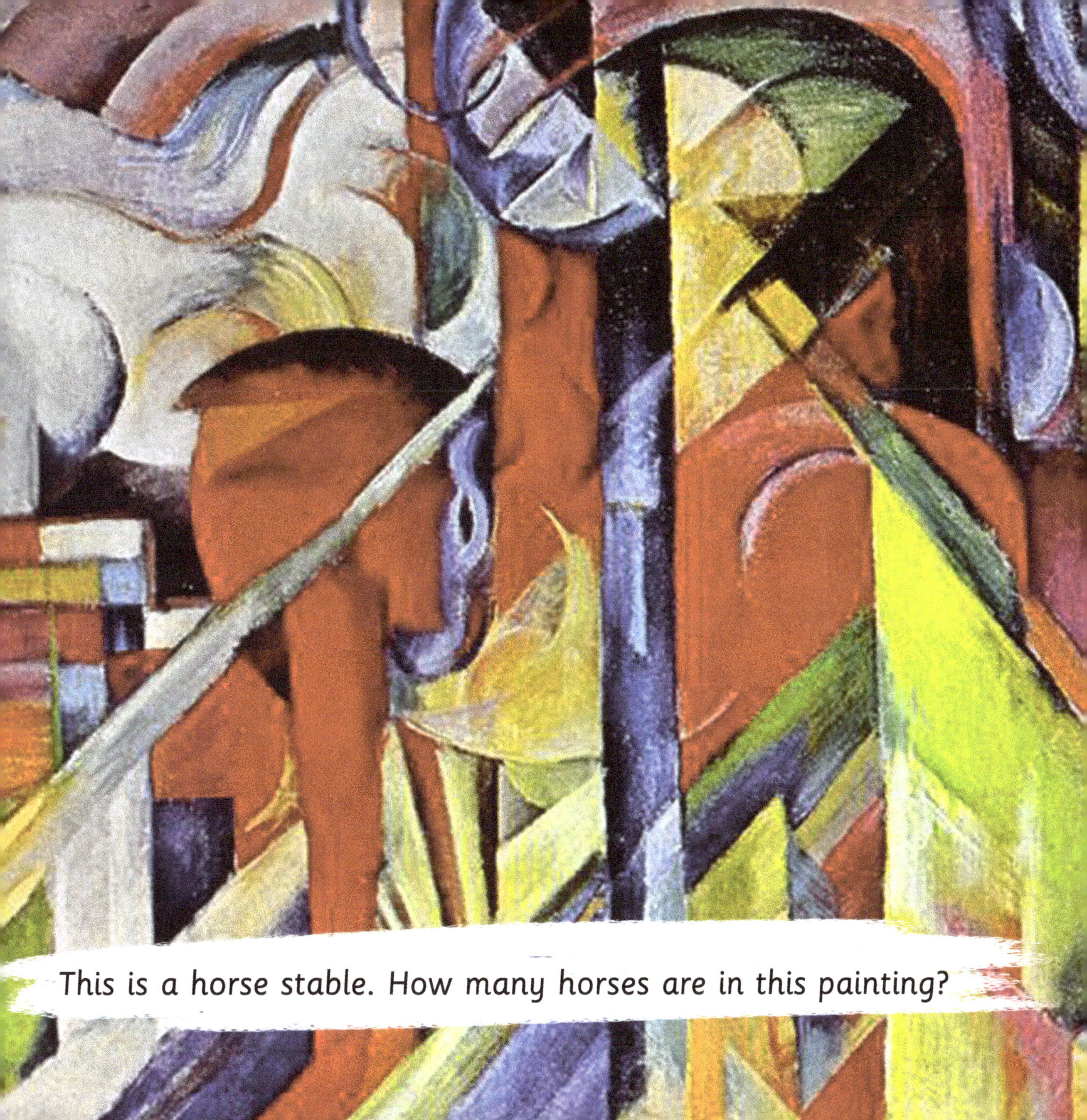

This is a horse stable. How many horses are in this painting?

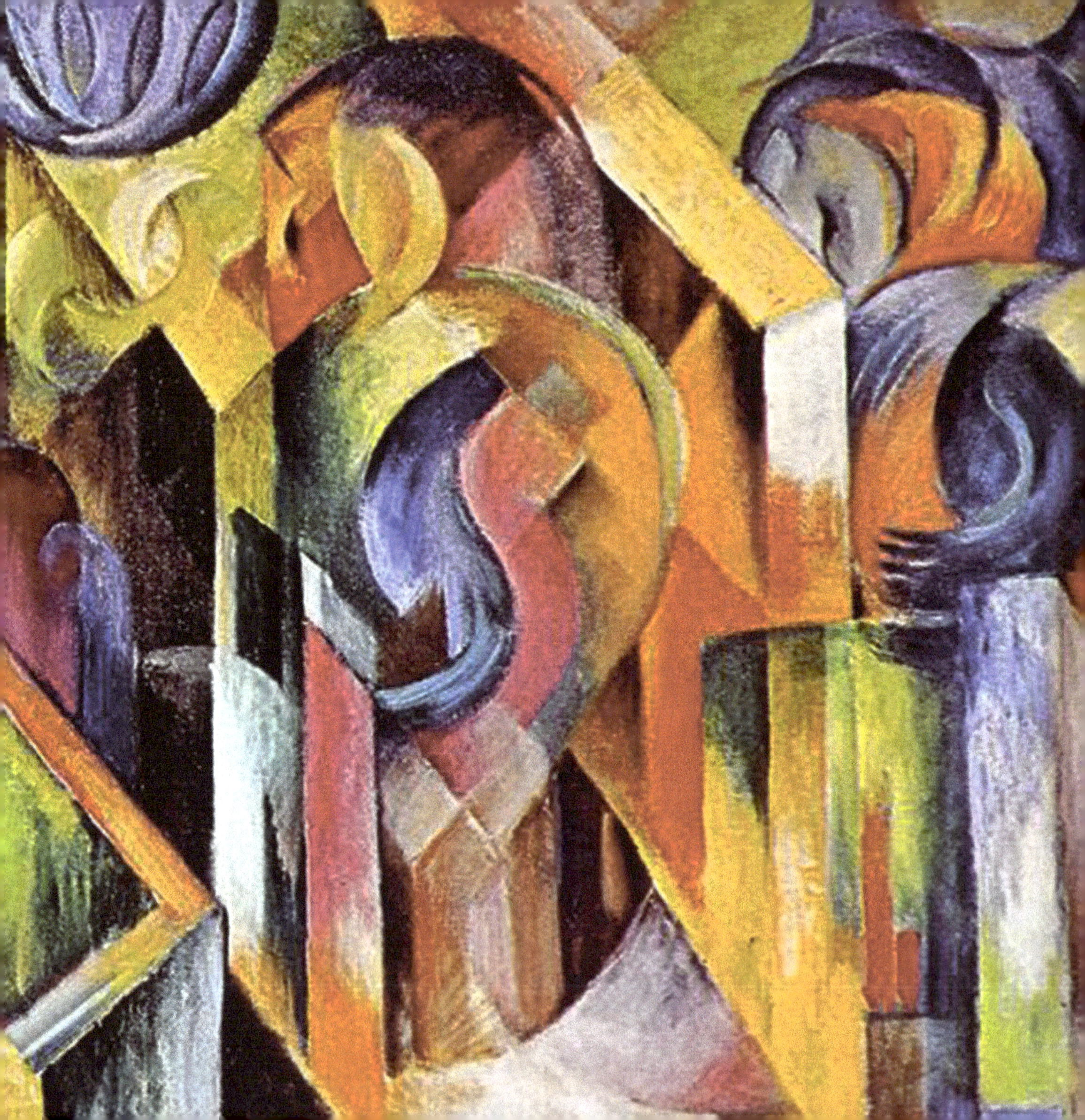

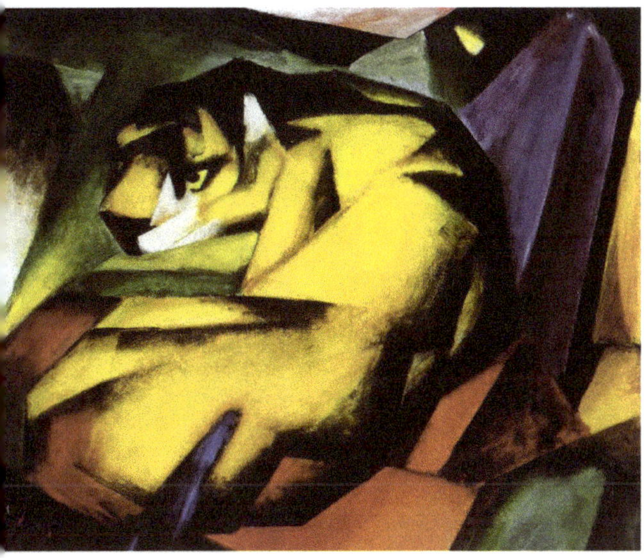

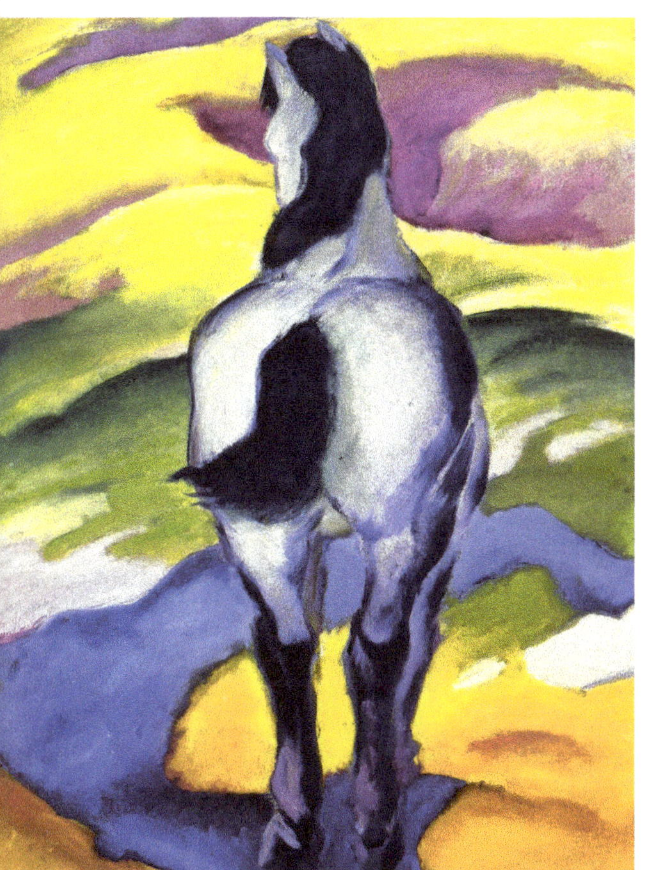

Franz Marc was a famous
painter. He loved to paint animals.

Cats and yellow dogs.
Elephants and red tigers.
Monkeys and blue cows.

Do animals wear these colour skins?
Maybe not, said the painter.
What's outside, doesn't matter.
Colour is what we see!
Heart is what we feel!

Come ... see and see again.
Make friends with Franz's animals.
Paint and paint again ... like
Franz Marc!

Want to paint like Franz Marc?

1. Use bold colours.
2. Practise! Practise! Practise!
3. Be humble. Learn from others.

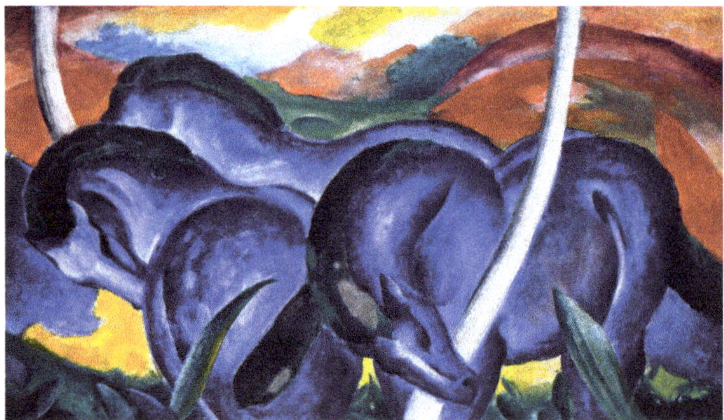

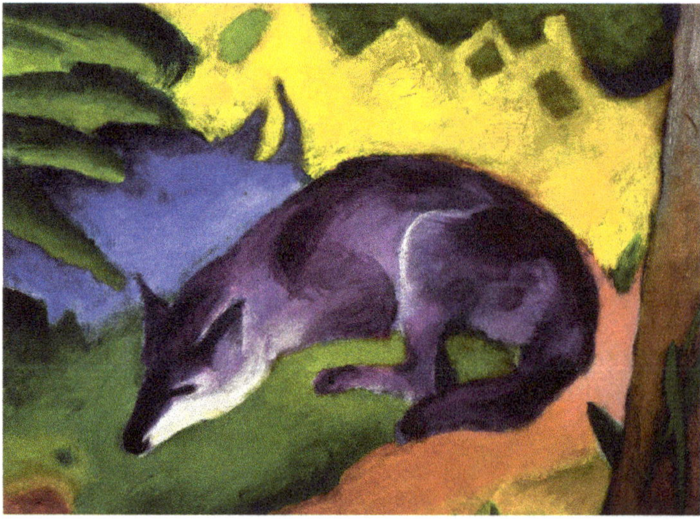

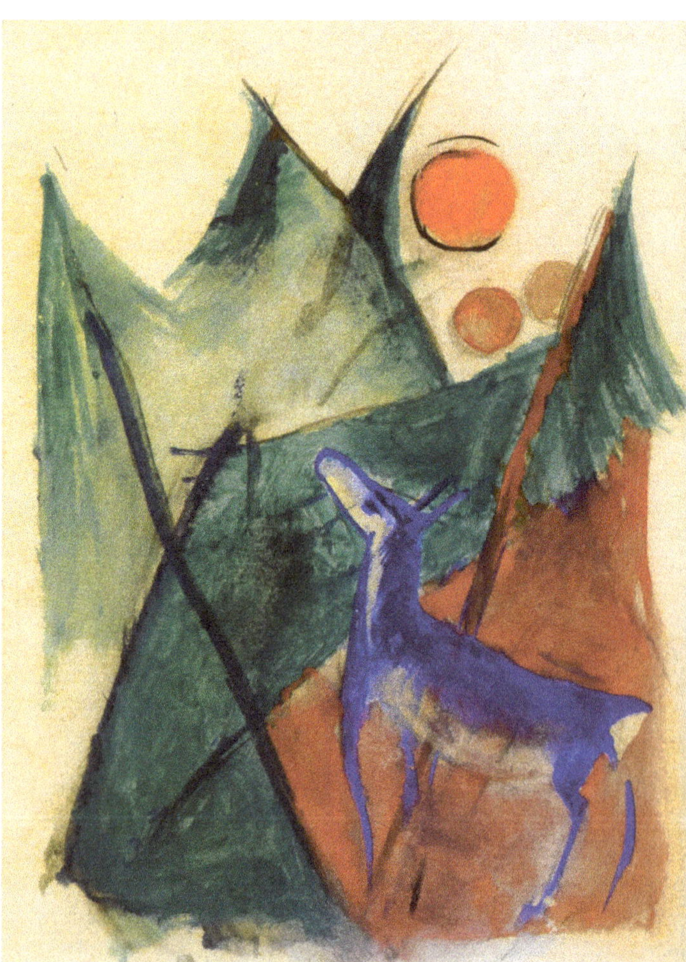

Think

Is the animal on the moon or on Earth, many years ago when there were no humans?

Ask

What if there were no more animals? No tigers, no fish, no birds, no dogs. Would anyone like that world?

Discuss

Animals like cows and elephants love to be in a group. Animals like tigers and turtles like being alone. Do you think we have this in common with animals?

Would you like to give this animal a friend?

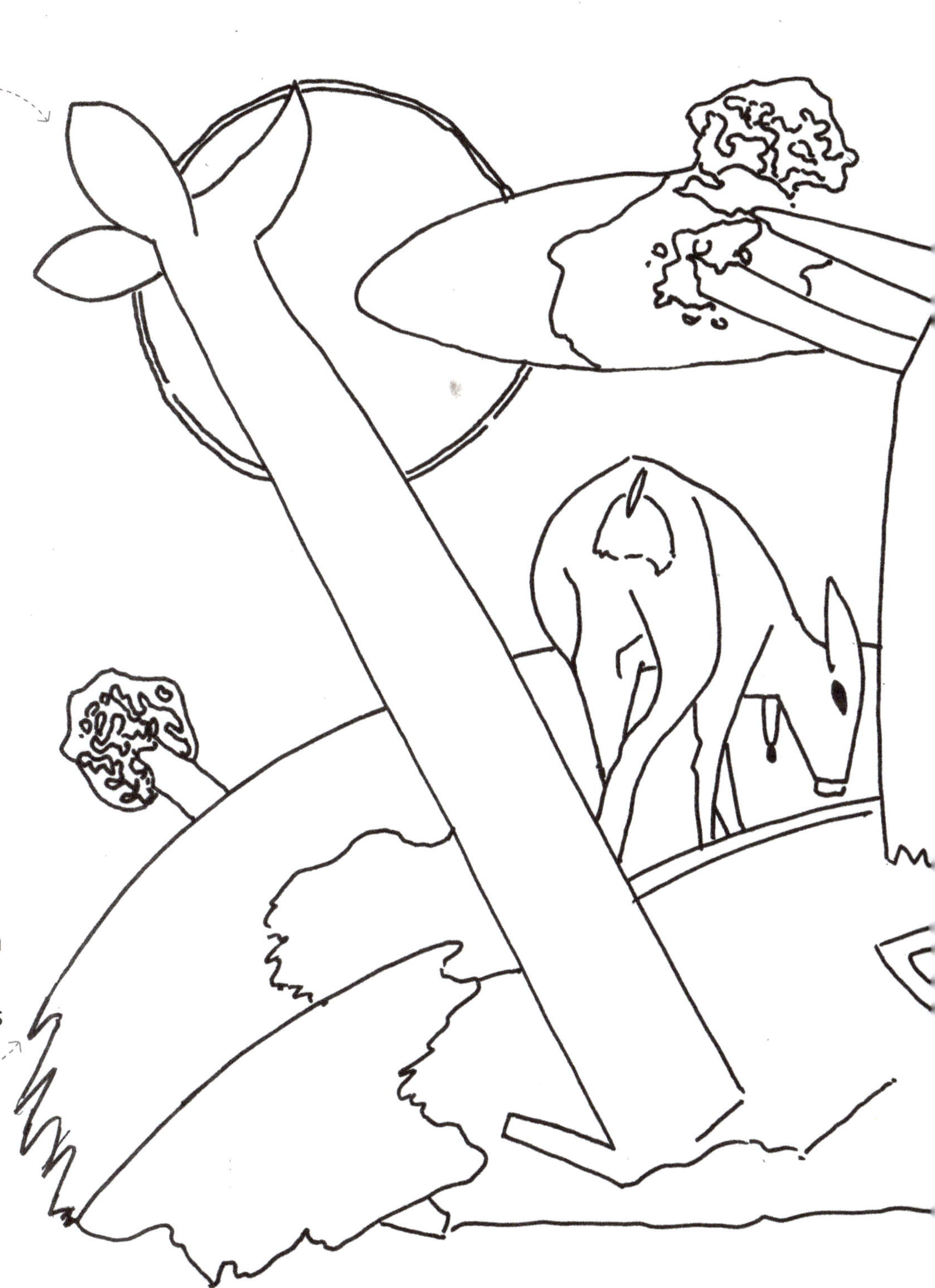

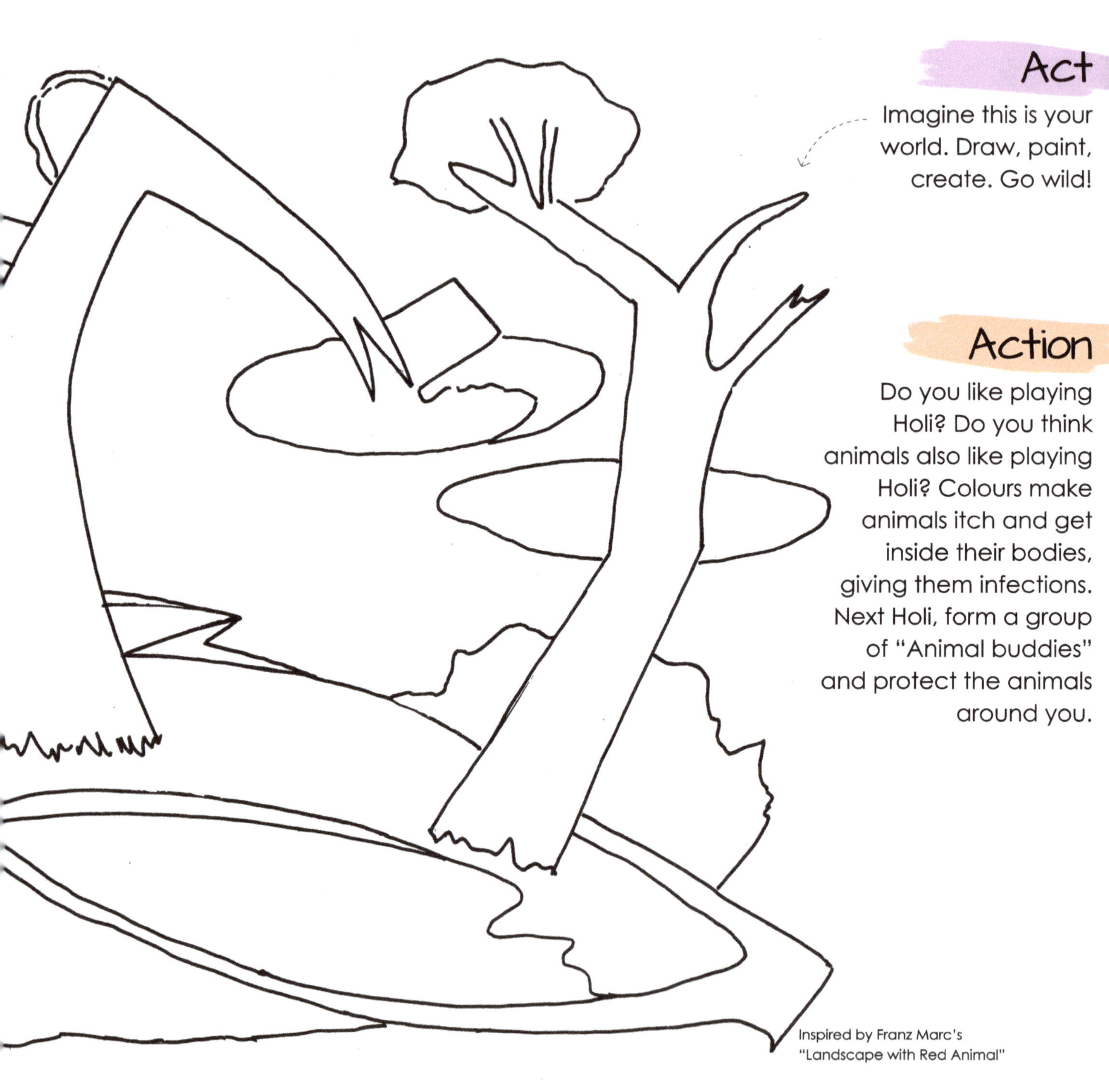

Act

Imagine this is your world. Draw, paint, create. Go wild!

Action

Do you like playing Holi? Do you think animals also like playing Holi? Colours make animals itch and get inside their bodies, giving them infections. Next Holi, form a group of "Animal buddies" and protect the animals around you.

Inspired by Franz Marc's "Landscape with Red Animal"

Geeta Dharmarajan loves writing for children. She started Katha in 1988 and has led the nonprofit since then. Creator of StoryPedagogy™ and other disruptive innovations for Katha, Geeta received the Padma Shri in 2012 for her pathbreaking work in literature and education. She was named "frugal innovator" by the Millennium Alliance, set up by the governments of India and the US; and co-winner of the Business Standard Social Entrepreneur of the Year for 2018.

Franz Marc was a painter. He was born in Germany. He loved colours. His father was a painter too. His mother looked after his father and him.

Franz loved to draw animals. He thought they were nice to one another, that they were like children. When he was 20 years old, Franz Marc began to study art at a college where he had excellent teachers. But, he continued to learn every day by seeing the paintings in museums. He would copy many paintings, to learn different styles. He also attended a lot of meetings where painters got together.

He died when he was 36 years old, during World War 1. But he created amazing art for all of us to see. And enjoy!

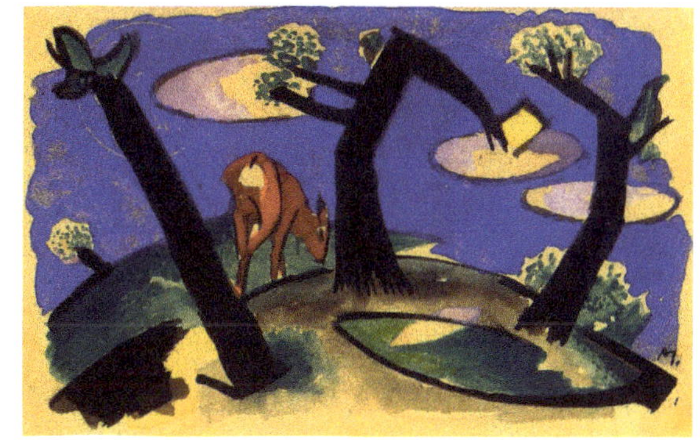

Landscape with Red Animal

Paintings courtesy of www.the-athenaeum.org

Cover painting: Cats, Red & White | **Paintings in the book:** Bull | Tiger in Jungle | Gazelles | Cows, Red, Green, Yellow | Monkey Frieze Pigs | Donkey Frieze | Bison in Winter | Jumping Horse | Cow and Sheep | Three Cats | Stables | Tigers | Blue Horse II The Large Blue Horses | Blue Deer in Landscape

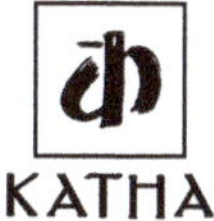

KATHA

First published by Katha, 2019

Printed in New Delhi

ISBN 978-93-88284-41-7

Our Mission: Every child reading well for fun and meaning!

KATHA is a registered nonprofit organization started in 1988. We work in the literacy to literature continuum. Devoted to enhancing the joys of reading amongst children and adults, we work with more than 1,00,000 children in poverty, to bring them to grade-level reading through quality books and interventions.

A3, Sarvodaya Enclave, Sri Aurobindo Marg, New Delhi 110 017

Phone: 4141 6600 . 4182 9998 . 2652 1752

E-mail: marketing@katha.org, Website: www.katha.org, www.books.katha.org

Ten per cent of sales proceeds from this book will support the quality education of children studying in Katha schools.

Katha regularly plants trees to replace the wood used in the making of its books.

make friends with painters through katha books!

Raza by Raza

SAYED HAIDER RAZA

A colourful journey of dots and squares, triangles and patterns. Meet Sayed Haider Raza and discover the artist within you!

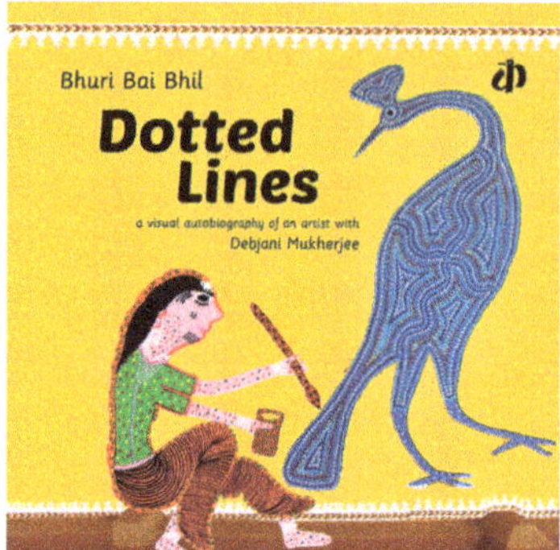

Dotted Lines

BHURI BAI BHIL WITH
DEBJANI MUHERJEE

Awesome art brings to life a heartwarming story of a girl from Madhya Pradesh as she becomes a Bhil artist.

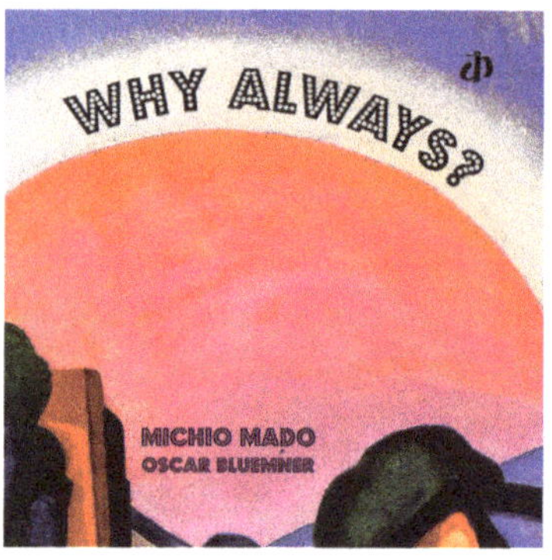

Why Always?

MICHIO MADO
ART BY OSCAR BLUEMNER

Katha brings together two nature lovers to fill your heart with joy and wonder.

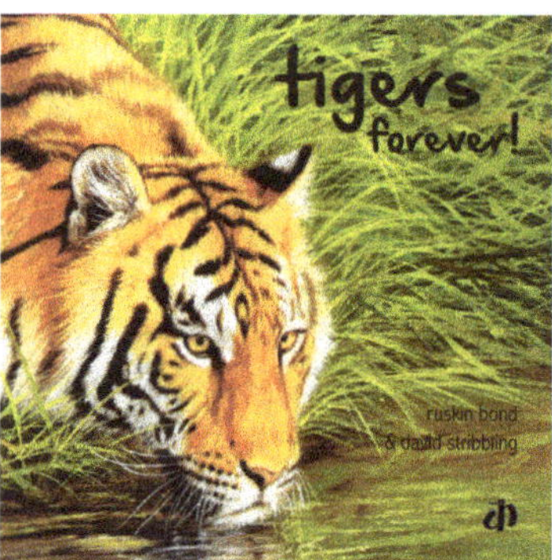

Tigers Forever!

RUSKIN BOND
ART BY DAVID STRIBBLING

Take a trip to the jungle to meet this spectacular animal, with every child's favourite Ruskin Bond and the lifelike paintings of David Stribbling.

www.ingramcontent.com/pod-product-compliance
Lightning Source LLC
LaVergne TN
LVHW060628110826
845147LV00015B/965

* 9 7 8 9 3 8 8 2 8 4 4 1 7 *